Roman Missal Companion

Table of Contents

INTRODUCTION

Archbishop J. Augustine Di Noia, O.P.
Secretary of the Congregation for Divine Worship
and the Discipline of the Sacraments

AFTER EIGHT YEARS OF WORK on the part of the Bishops' Conferences, the International Commission for English in the Liturgy, and the *Vox Clara* Committee of the Congregation for Divine Worship and the Discipline of the Sacraments, a new English translation of the Roman Missal has been published for use throughout the English-speaking world. Bishops and experts from the United States, Canada, England, Ireland, India, Australia, and anglophone African countries joined with the Congregation for Divine Worship in an intensive process involving the careful study of every line of the translation in order to ensure that the texts would be faithful to the Latin original and understandable in every region where English is the language of the sacred liturgy.

Christ Made Present

When Pope Benedict XVI received this new translation of the Roman Missal on April 28, 2010, he acknowledged the "great labor" expended in "the preparation and translation of texts that proclaim the truth of our redemption in Christ, the Incarnate Word of God… I welcome the news that the English translation of the Roman Missal will soon be ready for publication, so that the texts you have worked so hard to prepare may be proclaimed in the liturgy that is celebrated across the anglophone world. Through these sacred texts and the actions that accompany them, Christ will be made present and active in the midst of his people" (*Notitiae* 47 [2010], 157-8). The Holy Father was delighted that the English-speaking bishops of the world had been able to agree on a single version of the Roman Missal for global use. Given the importance of the English language in all sectors of international communication and the absolute centrality of the sacred liturgy to the life of every Catholic community, this immensely significant achievement will serve the unity in faith and the communion in charity of the universal Church.

Unity in Faith

That the one Catholic Church praises God in the Holy Mass using the same words is both an expression and a confirmation of the unity in faith which underlies the communion in charity that is essential to the life of the Church. When Latin was the language in which the Mass was celebrated in every part of the Catholic world in the Latin Rite (and commonly used sacred languages in the various Oriental Catholic rites), unity in faith and worship was not an issue. But since the Catholic Church of the Latin Rite authorized the celebration of the Mass in a range of vernacular languages after the Second Vatican Council, the bishops of the world and the Holy See have been concerned to ensure the continuity and universality – in other words, the *catholicity* – of the celebration of the Mass through the use of accurate and authentic translations of the Roman Missal.

The introduction of vernacular translations of the Roman Missal was, of course, a tremendous boon. Its purpose was to enhance the full and active participation of the faithful in the Eucharistic Sacrifice of the Mass – "uniting ourselves to Christ… who offers himself to the Father…, who receives the gift of God…, who loves the Father above all else; uniting ourselves to Christ in praise of the Father, uniting ourselves to Christ in thanksgiving, uniting ourselves to Christ in his very attitude before the Father," to use the words of Cardinal Antonio Cañizares, prefect of the Congregation for Divine Worship (*Notitiae* 47 [2010], 151). The more fully we understand the words of the sacred liturgy, the more confidently can we unite ourselves in faith, through the power of the Holy Spirit, to the perfect worship of the Father rendered by the eternal sacrifice of his Son, Jesus Christ our Lord, and thus attain at least a measure of the full and active participation in the Mass that the Church so keenly desires for all of us.

Quality and Authenticity

It is for this reason that the bishops and the Holy See exercise such a high degree of vigilance over the quality and authenticity of the vernacular translations of the sacred liturgy in use throughout the world. Every translation in use over the past forty years is being subjected to a thorough re-evaluation according to newly articulated principles provided by the Holy See to ensure fidelity to the Latin text of the Roman Missal as well as a truly sacral tone suitable to the worship of God. The new English Missal is one of the first among many new vernacular translations that have been or will soon be published after receiving the approval of the Holy See.

With this splendid *Roman Missal Companion*, MAGNIFICAT has responded to the pressing need to which Pope Benedict XVI drew special attention when he encouraged the *Vox Clara*

Committee to prepare "for the reception of the new translation by clergy and lay faithful. Many will find it hard to adjust to unfamiliar texts after nearly forty years of continuous use of the previous translation. The change will need to be introduced with due sensitivity, and the opportunity for catechesis that it presents will need to be firmly grasped. I pray that in this way any risk of confusion or bewilderment will be averted, and the change will serve instead as a springboard for a renewal and a deepening of Eucharistic devotion all over the English-speaking world" (*Notitiae* 47 [2010], 158). The publication of the English translation of the *Roman Missal, Third Edition* thus provides an occasion, not only for an explanation of the new language that will henceforth be used in the celebration of the Holy Mass across the English-speaking Catholic world, but more importantly for a catechesis that will deepen our understanding of and participation in the sacred mysteries which are Christ's permanent gift to his Church. This MAGNIFICAT *Roman Missal Companion* makes a significant contribution to the achievement of these compelling objectives.

PART I

EDITORIAL

Father Peter John Cameron, O.P.

B Y TRAINING, I AM A PLAYWRIGHT. Once in graduate school, a pro named Eric Overmyer came to speak to us about the craft of writing. The dramatist had authored the most widely produced play in the United States at that time, a comedy entitled *On the Verge, or the Geography of Yearning* (he has gone on to write hit television shows). Eric Overmyer is a fanatic about language, of which his play is a magnificent celebration. In the production notes to *On the Verge*, the playwright makes this statement: "Rhythm and sound are sense. [The phrase] 'One tiny *Times* item' is very different from 'One tiny *Times* article.'" I have always been struck by this simple but seminal distinction. The way we say things matters. It changes how we think and how we feel. In a world of myriad synonyms, finding "the right word" remains a considerably more intricate and involved process than one may imagine. It entails hitting upon a certain rhythm and sound that renders a certain special sense. We know it when we hear it.

Sense and Reference

The Church has made a new translation of the Mass in order to give us a more sublime sense of the liturgy. In this, the rhythm and sound of the *Roman Missal, Third Edition* plays a key role. The twentieth-century philosopher Paul Ricœur wrote: "To understand a text is to follow its movement from sense to reference, from what it says to what it talks about." In other words, good communication happens when the sense – the concrete and intentional phrasing of a text – leads us to something beyond the words: to the reality the words are talking about. The newly wrought literary sense in the *Roman Missal, Third Edition* enables us to experience the meaning and truth of the Mystery more profoundly. That design of the new Missal is in the design of its words.

Responding to Secularism

There is another reason for the new translation. The Church wants to restore to her worship a heightened sense of the sacred. The wisdom of this move is something the theologian Wolfhart Pannenberg called for in an authoritative article he published in 1996 entitled "How to Think about Secularism." There he wrote:

> The absolutely worst way to respond to the challenge of secularism is to adapt to secular standards in language, thought, and way of life. If members of a secularist society turn to religion at all, they do so because they are looking for something other than what that culture already provides. It is counterproductive to offer them religion in a secular mode that is carefully trimmed in order not to offend their secular sensibilities… What people look for in religion is a plausible alternative, or at least a complement, to life in a secularist society. Religion that is "more of the same" is not likely to be very interesting… When message and ritual are accommodated, when the offending edges are removed, people are invited to suspect that the clergy do not really believe anything so very distinctive.

Souls Communicating

The Church's response to such secularist trends is to present a new translation of the Mass that is aesthetically rich. For nothing transforms us like beauty. The philosopher Jacques Maritain wrote that "the moment one touches a transcendental [like the beautiful], one touches being itself, a likeness of God,… that which ennobles and delights our life… Only in this way do [people] escape from the individuality in which matter encloses them… They observe each other without seeing each other, each one of them infinitely alone… But let one touch the good and love the true… the beautiful…, then contact is made, souls communicate."

The aim of the new translation is to bring forth the sublime in the liturgy much along the lines that the third-century Longinus defined it: "Sublimity is a certain distinction and excellence in expression. The effect of elevated language upon an audience is not persuasion but transport." Or even better in the words of Blessed John Paul II: "Ultimately, the mystery of language brings us back to *the inscrutable mystery of God himself.*"

Father Peter John Cameron, o.p., is the editor-in-chief of Magnificat *and the editor of* Benedictus: Day by Day with Pope Benedict XVI.

Liturgical Language and Communion

Father Bernard Mulcahy, O.P.

THE APOSTLES "were all persevering unanimously in prayer with the women and Mary, the Mother of Jesus" (Acts 1: 14, author's translation). Scripture emphasizes that the Apostolic Church acted and prayed *homothumadon*, that is, in unison of mind and deed. Explaining this in reference to the liturgy handed down from the Apostles, Saint Cyprian writes in his *Treatise on the Lord's Prayer*: "They were with one mind continuing steadfastly in prayer, declaring alike by their constancy and unity in prayer that God, who makes men of one mind to dwell in a home, does not admit into the divine and eternal home any except those who are of one mind in prayer" (chapter 7).

The revised English translation of our Roman Missal gives us a chance to purify and deepen our communion in the Body of Christ, the Catholic Church, in two ways. First, it invites us to attend more closely to the words and spirit of the apostolic tradition of our sacred liturgy. Second, it confronts us with the need to work at our common prayer and approach the liturgy as disciples rather than masters.

Like the other sacraments, the Mass was instituted by Jesus Christ. Like the other sacraments, it comes down to us, through the Apostles, in several distinct forms. There are Greek Catholic liturgies, Syriac Catholic liturgies, Coptic

Catholic liturgies, and others within the communion of the Catholic Church. Each apostolic liturgical lineage embodies the Gospel and, kept alive by the Holy Spirit, puts its people into the communion of Catholic prayer. The particular heritage to which the largest number of Catholics happens to belong is the Latin Rite, with the Latin language as its native tongue.

Coming Closer

Like the other Catholic Churches, our Latin Church has begun using translations into vernacular languages. Human words, of course, cannot of themselves deliver salvation and the new life of the kingdom. Only one word, the Word incarnate, can do this. Nonetheless the words we use together in prayer and in the sacred liturgy matter a great deal. If we no longer know the mother tongue of our church, then a translation is very valuable for putting us in touch with the mind of our church and of the whole Church. The revised English Missal can deepen our communion precisely by forming us more closely to the apostolic patrimony of our rite. To some extent this will happen unconsciously, as we assimilate the words and meanings of the words used at Mass. Our progress can also be deliberate: taking care to study and savor the words of the liturgy, with care to learn *why* the Apostles' successors – our pope and bishops – prefer a revised English translation, will help even more. Even if we never or rarely celebrate our Latin liturgy in the Latin language, we can at least come closer to the shared Latin heritage and to a more full Catholic understanding by using a better translation.

Re-learning

The second advantage to the revised translation is in the work it asks us to do. And here we might distinguish between the work of our priests and other liturgical ministers on one hand, and then of all the people at Mass on the other hand.

For priests and other ministers of the liturgy, the new English Missal is an opportunity to re-learn and then to do what the Roman Rite requires. We all know that after Vatican II the Mass was often celebrated more informally and with more self-expression by the celebrant. Without being overly rigid, we do greatly need this reminder that in the liturgy we are ministers, servants. We have our roles in the Mass in obedience to the Master, and must not obtrude ourselves into everyone's attention. The principal actor at Mass is Christ crucified, and having to pay closer attention to a new Missal can help put us in our places.

One Mind and Heart

For all the English-speaking Latin Catholic faithful, the new Missal is a challenge that demands our time, practice, and patience. It is true that praying with these new words *interiorly* – "active participation" – can happen right away. Praying with one mind and heart at Mass in English or Latin or any language is essentially the fruit of faith and charity, not of editors or translators. To chant or recite our new liturgical words *outwardly* with one voice, however, is going to take time. Here love, patience, and modesty – a subdued voice – are necessary if we are going to relax into the new rhythm of words together. Again the words of Saint Cyprian, from the same passage, are apt: "When we meet together and celebrate the divine sacrifices with God's priest, we ought to be mindful of modesty and discipline." For all of us the new English Missal gives us a chance to encounter the words of the liturgy afresh, to become liturgical novices or children again, and to learn from Christ and his Apostles.

Father Bernard Mulcahy, O.P., is a Dominican priest of the Province of Saint Joseph and a theologian. He is the author of a number of theological works, including "The Authority of Scripture in Sacramental Theology," *which he co-authored with (Archbishop) J. Augustine Di Noia, O.P.*

On the Art of Translation

Professor Anthony Esolen

IT IS AN HONOR FOR ME, and a great delight, to help to introduce my fellow English-speaking Catholics to the new translation of the Holy Mass.

Why a New Translation

"Why should there be a translation at all?" some of the faithful may wonder. Well, the new Order of Mass – not the so-called "Latin Mass," more properly named the Tridentine Rite Mass, which was said in all countries before the Second Vatican Council recommended the use of the vernacular and revised the structure and the language of the Mass – is written in Latin, as are all the prayers used at Mass, for every day of the year, and for every purpose for which a Mass is said. These texts must be translated, then, from the original Latin into English and all the other vernacular languages of the world. Thus, when the priest says, "The Lord be with you," the response in the vernacular languages has simply translated the Latin *"Et cum spiritu tuo,"* "And with your spirit," so that in Sweden the response is just that, *"Och med din ande,"* as it is in German, *"Und mit deinem Geist,"* as it is in Italian, *"E con il tuo spirito."* The new translation in English, then, is meant to bring our prayers closer not only to the original Latin, but to what our brothers and sisters throughout the world have long been saying in *their* languages.

Meaning for Meaning

Granted, then, that the Mass must be translated, I should like to begin with a brief discussion of the challenges that a translator must face, particularly if he is translating something other than ordinary speech – poetry, for instance, or prayer.

It is one of the maxims of translation that we are supposed to render meaning for meaning, and not simply word for word. We are not to hang ourselves by the rope of literalism. The Vatican's guidelines for liturgical translation (*Liturgiam Authenticam*) state as much. And the maxim is true, if what is said in the original language is already to be understood in a figurative way. So, for example, someone learning German will be taught that if you want to say "Goodbye," you say, "*Auf Wiedersehen,*" or, in common speech, simply "*Wiedersehen.*" The meanings are "equivalent" in their situations of use. If you're waving to friends at a train station, you will say "Goodbye" in Boston and "*Auf Wiedersehen*" in Berlin. That's so, even though "Goodbye" is an old contraction of the phrase "God be with you," and "*Auf Wiedersehen*" is a contraction of the very different phrase "Until we see one another again." Its closest English counterpart would be "See you later," but the jauntiness and familiarity of that phrase would often be quite inappropriate. If a German man shakes the hand of the Pope in the Vatican and says, "*Auf Wiedersehen,*" we had better translate it as simply "Goodbye."

So of course it is true that a translation cannot be slavishly bound to the literal, but that is only because the original language itself is not always used in a literal sense, or because what works in the grammar of one language does not work in the grammar of another, so that words have to be supplied, or combined, or rearranged. When in the preface to the liturgy of the Eucharist, the priest calls out, *"Sursum corda,"* he is using a phrase in Latin that has no verb. *Sursum* is an adverb without an exact counterpart in English. It means, roughly, "up from below," so that the phrase, if we translated without an ear for our own language, might be rendered, "Hearts up from below." But that does not make much sense. We need a verb. So our translators have justifiably supplied a verb and even a possessive pronoun to make the phrase clear: "Lift up your hearts."

Keeping Close to the Literal: Reason One

And yet – granting all that – it is better to err on the side of the literal. There are, as I see them, three reasons for this. The first is that the task of the translator demands humility. If I am translating the poet Dante, I must assume that Dante knew what he was doing, and that I am not supposed to intrude my personal poetic sensibility or my philosophy or my theology into the work. Indeed, the reverse is true. It is Dante's poetic sensibility and philosophy and theology that I must struggle to reveal. I must take as my own the frank confession of John the Baptist: "He must increase, and I must decrease." If the Order of the Mass has the people responding to the priest, *"Et cum spiritu tuo,"* I cannot say to myself, "I should prefer a different response." I cannot say, "I wish to ensure that there is no felt distinction between the people and the priest." I am not hired to quarrel with the original. I am hired to submit to it. So now the people respond, "And with your spirit," and the mystery of the response, the prayer that God might animate the spirit of the man who leads us in prayer, justly remains.

Reason Two

The second reason for keeping close to the literal might seem, to a casual observer, to contradict what I have said above, and that is that a peculiar usage in one language *might not have a true counterpart* in another, and that it therefore might reveal something in reality that is obscured in the other. In other words, we might want a literal translation *precisely because we do not say things that way in our language*, but rather because the original helps us see what we might otherwise miss. Take for example Mary's reply to Gabriel, when the angel tells her that she will bear a son. "How can this be," she asks, "since I have had no relations with a man?" Now that is how we currently hear it translated in our lectionary, and if the purpose is simply to stress that Mary is a virgin, that is well enough. But the Greek in Luke's Gospel uses the verb "know" – "I know not man" – and not because the Greeks used it that way, but because the Hebrews did. That verb is far richer than the rather technical phrase "to have relations with." We are, in an instant, brought back to the first man and woman, when Adam "knew" his wife, and she bore him a son. And we are reminded, in a gentle way, that the union of man and woman was never meant to be merely the union of flesh, or the establishment of some "relation" or other, but the union of whole beings, a union of intimate knowledge.

Reason Three

The third reason is a corollary of the two above. If my task is to submit to the original, and if the original often shows me what my own language sometimes obscures, then a close examination of the literal words may *unlock the figurative meaning beneath*. That is, I am not preferring the figurative to the literal, but am *revealing the figurative through the literal*. Take for example our response to the priest's call, "Behold the Lamb of God, who takes away the sins of the world." It is the literal rendering, and not the more distant rendering we have grown accustomed to, that opens out to us the profound analogy between ourselves and the centurion in the Gospel, who begged Jesus to heal his servant. "Lord," we say, repeating the centurion's words, "I am not worthy that you should enter under my roof." The Lord's offering to go to the centurion's house is a foreshadowing of his entering the house of our body, in the form of bread. His is the action, his is the offer; he is the one who wishes to take up his dwelling within us.

A Language of Prayer

The translation we are adopting is, I affirm, more *faithful* to the original, both in its accuracy and in its humble and generous submission. And this leads me to a crucial point about the language of faith. Consider the difference between a grand piano and a toy piano, or between a cornet and a harmonica. You may play a C on each instrument, and in a certain sense they will all be playing one note; you will recognize the pitch as the same. But it would be absurd to suppose that there is no difference – and indeed all the difference in the world – between the grand piano and the toy piano, or between the cornet and the harmonica. The grand piano is an instrument of surpassing power; the toy piano is but a child's half-comical imitation. The cornet is an instrument for proclaiming the approach of a king; the harmonica, for a lonely farmer boy out in the fields, musing about the lovely girl in the village nearby.

As in music, so in language. There are many instruments that play in English: consider the rough banter of boys on a street corner; the colorless formality of an office memorandum; the tender phrases of a love letter, tinged with nostalgia; the intricacy of poetry in meter and rhyme. So the question is not simply, "How do we translate this Latin into English?" but "What instrument in English is best for this instrument in Latin?" How do we translate the language of prayer? And there is a language of prayer.

I have heard it said that when Jesus prayed, he used the common language of the people. The implication is that there should be no real difference between the style of our prayers and the style, say, of our letters to the editor. But the premise is wrong, and so is the conclusion. The fact is, there was no such thing as one "common language of the people." That is because, as I've suggested, language is a many splendored thing. The farmer in old Quebec speaks in a courtly way to his wife – but not so to his horse or his dog. A soldier writing home to his beloved allows himself flights of fancy that would be laughed at in the barracks. Every language too has a sacral register. That was true of the Aramaic that Jesus spoke. More than that, when Jesus gathered with his disciples to celebrate the sacred feasts, or when he read in the synagogues, it was not Aramaic that he read, and not Aramaic psalms that he sang, but Hebrew, the ancient language of his people.

The Structure of Sentences

That concern for the sacred character of our worship at Mass is made manifest in another way, beyond the choice of words and the determination to render into English the beauty of the Latin. It is made manifest in the length and the structure of the sentences. This too is something that calls for explanation.

When we read, we can do all kinds of things that help us make sense of a difficult passage. We can insert a bookmark and put the book down for a while. We can turn the page back to something we had read before. We can glance ahead to see if an explanation is coming. We can read the passage over again. But we can do none of these things while we are *listening* to a speech. Oratory, in other words, cannot work like straight prose. It requires the linking devices of oral poetry. It requires repetition of key words, parallel structures in grammar and sense, balance of idea with idea and image with image, and – something that people unused to oral poetry do not suspect – a minimum of full stops that interrupt the flow of declamation and meaning. That is why Homer, who composed his great poems the *Iliad* and the *Odyssey* using his mind and his voice and his ear, and not his hand and his eye, since these poems would not be written down for centuries, and since, as tradition has it, he was blind – it is why the great Homer employs long, flowing, delicately balanced sentences, with many repeated forms and phrases, so that the work could be *heard*, and, more important than that, *remembered*. That is why when Martin Luther King addressed the hundreds of thousands on the Mall in Washington, he spoke in a series of long sentences with all the balance and repetition of a Jeremiah or Isaiah, and why so many of us still remember what he said was the vision of his dream.

In oratory, as in oral poetry, every full stop is a breach, and runs the risk of losing the ear and the memory. Four consecutive simple declarative sentences are, taken singly, easier to hear and to remember than one long and complex sentence would be, but taken together they are like disconnected boxcars bumping into each other on a track. So there is an eminently practical reason, and an aesthetic reason, for translating a long sentence of oratory as a long sentence of oratory. But there is still more. The elements of such sentences *belong together*. When we separate them into their own sentences, we lose the theological connections between them. They no longer form parts of an intricate whole. Indeed, we are often reduced to the awkward position of informing God of what he already knows, stopping in our tracks, and then praying for something that occurs to us as an afterthought. That is not the way of the new translation.

Let me give a prime example. In the new translation, most of the prefaces to the Liturgy of the Eucharist consist of a single sentence, between the declaration of the priest that it is right for us to praise God, and his summoning us to join the angels and archangels in their hymn of praise. Typically, an opening clause after the pronoun "who" reminds us of what God has done for us – rather than reporting the information back to God; and that is followed by a prayer that is to be considered in light of what God has done, or a reflection upon the meaning of God's action. Here, for example, is the central portion of the Preface for the Assumption of Mary:

For today the Virgin Mother of God
was assumed into heaven
as the beginning and image
of your Church's coming to perfection
and a sure sign of hope and comfort to your pilgrim people;
rightly you would not allow her
to see the corruption of the tomb
since from her own body she marvelously brought forth
your incarnate Son, the Author of all life.

Notice, in this lovely prayer, that we begin and end with our minds devoted to the Motherhood of Mary, as is right and just for this solemn feast. Notice too that what is in the middle is deftly balanced, one truth reflecting upon another, so that the Assumption of Mary is an image of the raising of the Church and of all her pilgrims. Both are a reflection of the Resurrection of Jesus in his glorified body, Jesus, to whom the Church applies the words of the Psalm: "You would not let your holy one see corruption."

Steeped in Scripture

And that leads me to the last but perhaps most important point. It is astonishing how steeped in Scripture the prayers of the Mass are, how, for example, a passage from Saint Paul will be placed alongside a passage from the Psalms, effortlessly interwoven, to make a profound theological point, or to see our Christian prayer as springing from and elevating the prayers of the children of Israel. It is no exaggeration to say that even the relatively short prayers before the Liturgy of the Word, the Collects, echo one or two passages in the Word of God. Every single Collect is delicately and wisely crafted to fit the season and the day. The new translation unmuffles that Word of God, so that we can hear it once again in all of our prayers, and so that we can glimpse the great work of sacred art that the Mass is. It is an art whose language comes from God himself, and yet it is an art for everyone. Our heads have been anointed with oil; our cups overflow.

So when we pray in this translation, let us not be embarrassed by beauty, by intricacy, by elevation, by mystery, by the potency of repetition, by fullness of heart and of expression. Let us instead consider every word of the Latin to be like the wine at Cana, and let us be grateful for translators who humbled themselves to accept that wine, without desiring to translate it back into water.

PART II

A Key to the Commentary

Professor Anthony Esolen

THE PURPOSE OF THE FOLLOWING COMMENTARY is to reveal some of the richness of the Order of the Mass as it has now been translated into English. What I have done is to flag certain passages for comment, for six principal reasons.

Six Reasons

First, the passages may differ significantly from what we have become accustomed to; for example, the response of the people to the elevation of the host, "Lord, I am not worthy that you should enter under my roof."

Second, they may restore words that had been omitted, or removed from their right place, as in the great sequence of verbs that begin the Gloria: "We praise you, we bless you, we adore you, we glorify you."

Third, they may translate more acutely and with greater attention to poetic specificity what had been left general and vague, as when the priest says that Jesus raised the chalice filled with "the fruit of the vine," or when, at the beginning of every Preface, the priest says that to give God thanks is "our duty and our salvation."

Fourth, they may resound more clearly with the language of Holy Scripture, as when in the third Eucharistic Prayer the priest says that God wishes to gather a people to himself "from the rising of the sun to its setting."

Fifth, they may revise an inaccuracy, as when, in the Creed, we replace the misleading phrase "seen and unseen," which suggests that we are considering things that some people happen to see or happen not to see, with the precise "visible and invisible," which affirms that God is the creator of things that are possible and impossible to be seen.

Sixth, they may raise the register of our prayer beyond the drab and the workaday to the sacral, as when we affirm that God does not merely "give" us good things, but "bestows" them upon all the world.

Restorations

It would be burdensome for the reader to have to persist through commentary on every single change, especially since many of them are repeated consistently from one part of the Mass to another, or from one Preface to the next. A few general comments, then, are in order here. The translators have strived, with impressive success, to be as faithful as possible to the meaning of the Latin text, and to the emphasis of the sentences as they are structured. The English reader can rely upon it that if the text includes what sounds like a new word of praise, for example "Blessed" in "Blessed ever-Virgin Mary," then that is because the Latin says exactly that, and the word *beata* is not omitted. Instances of such restoration are too numerous to comment upon them all. The reader should assume that the reasoning that applies to the first restoration of a word like "blessed" applies to all the rest. The reader may also rely upon what sounds like a new arrangement of elements in a sentence. The Gloria, for instance, is a poetic prayer of delicate balance, of variation within repetition. The translators therefore have restored the structure of the prayer, giving us once again our threefold proclamation of the Lamb of God who takes away the sins of the world, with the variant response "receive our prayer" bracketed, before and after, with the more fundamental "have mercy on us."

The translators have also attempted to retain something of the language of petition. They have done so, in my opinion, with a good deal of modesty. One will not meet, on every page, words such as "beseech," "implore," "beg," "supplicate," and "entreat," but they have restored words that remind us that we are praying to God, and not ordering him about. This restoration is perhaps most noticeable in the Collects, the prayers the priest says before the Liturgy of the Word. The Latin *quaesumus*, for example, very common in the Collects, is usually translated simply as "we pray," as a parenthetical clause, as in the original – and I believe with the gentle rhetorical effect of causing us to pause, before we announce our petition, to acknowledge that we are praying, and not demanding. It is at once more reverent and more personal than the bald verb would be. Note the difference between these two openings for the Collect of the First Sunday of Advent:

> All-powerful God, increase our strength of will for doing good...

> Grant your faithful, we pray, almighty God, the resolve to run forth to meet your Christ...

The second is a genuine translation of what the prayer really says, but, more than that, it possesses a poetic modulation in its own right; it seeks to do more than to declare a desire: it seeks to touch the heart. And much of that modulation comes from the faithful rendering of those two little words "we pray."

Use of Sacred Scripture

The commentary is, I hope, rewardingly rich in Scriptural references. For these, I have used as my primary text the New American Bible (NAB, copyright 1986; Psalms 1970) because it is reasonably close to the text of the lectionary used at Mass. But often it is clear that the translators are using Scriptural language that is not to be found in the NAB. The most notable example, perhaps, is their rendering of the traditional blessing on Ash Wednesday: "Remember that you are dust, and unto dust you shall return." The NAB has it as "dirt." So in many cases I have had recourse to an older translation, either the Revised Standard Version, Catholic Edition, or, when that too does not "pick up" the Scriptural language the translators have used, the Authorized King James Version. These will be noted as RSV or KJV.

I have commented here upon the Order of the Mass, including the four principal Eucharistic Prayers.

THE INTRODUCTORY RITES

■ *Priest:* **In the name of the Father, and of the Son, and of the Holy Spirit.**

■■ *People:* **Amen.**

• FORM A •

■ The grace of our Lord Jesus Christ,
and the love of God,
and the communion of the Holy Spirit
be with you all.

• FORM B •

■ Grace to you and peace from God our Father
and the Lord Jesus Christ.

• FORM C •

■ The Lord be with you.

COMMENTARY

...and the communion of the Holy Spirit: The word "communion" replaces "fellowship." The word is a more exact rendering of the Latin *communicatio*, which suggests not simply a settled state of love, but the dynamic act of sharing or imparting that love. The Holy Spirit imparts to us the same love that is given and received by the Persons of the Trinity. We are called to enter that communion, that life of love. The blessing is taken word for word from the conclusion of Saint Paul's second Letter to the Corinthians.

Grace to you and peace from God our Father and the Lord Jesus Christ: The precise words of Saint Paul, greeting the church at Philippi (Phil 1: 2). The order of the sentence is suggestive. The priest prays that we will be granted *grace*, which is the free gift of God's love, and without which we can do nothing of genuine merit, nothing that makes manifest the theological virtues of faith, hope, and charity. It is this grace, if we accept it, that brings us into friendship with God, who alone can grant us *peace*. Therefore the emphasis of the blessing is first of all on that grace. It is as if there were a prime blessing within a blessing: "Grace to you!" exclaims the priest.

■■ And with your spirit.

• PENITENTIAL ACT •

■ Brethren (brothers and sisters),
   let us acknowledge our sins,
and so prepare ourselves
   to celebrate the sacred mysteries.

And with your spirit: Our reply is formal and sacral, and indeed a prayer that dates back to the earliest years of the Church. We pray that the Lord may uphold our priest, not because he is better than we are, but so that he, human though he be, may serve us in his priestly capacity as an embodiment of Jesus, wedded to his bride, the Church. Saint Paul often uses the word "spirit" to refer to the core of a person's emotional being, what we might call the heart: so it is that to pray in tongues is to "pray with the spirit" (1 Cor 14: 15). We are asking, then, that the Lord will shower his gifts upon the spirit of the priest, so that he may help to build us up into one body. So Saint Paul bids farewell to all the churches of Galatia: "The grace of our Lord Jesus Christ be with your spirit" (Gal 6: 18), and to his beloved disciple, the bishop Saint Timothy: "The Lord be with your spirit" (2 Tm 4: 22).

Brethren, let us acknowledge our sins,/ and so prepare ourselves to celebrate the sacred mysteries: An exact translation of the Latin. With the word "brethren," the priest and the people are united in prayer to the Father of us all. We *acknowledge our sins*, not merely our failures, because a sin is more than a failure, it is a turn away from God. So we admit those sins, precisely that we may be prepared to celebrate the mysteries of forgiveness. The language is that of the powerful penitential Psalm 51, the *Miserere*: "For I acknowledge my offense, and my sin is before me always" (51: 5).

• Form A •

I confess to almighty God
and to you, my brothers and sisters,
that I have greatly sinned,
in my thoughts and in my words,
in what I have done and in what I have failed to do,

We strike our breast during the next two lines:

through my fault, through my fault,
through my most grievous fault;
therefore I ask blessed Mary ever-Virgin,
all the Angels and Saints,
and you, my brothers and sisters,
to pray for me to the Lord our God.

• Form B •

■ Have mercy on us, O Lord.
■ ■ For we have sinned against you.
■ Show us, O Lord, your mercy.
■ ■ **And grant us your salvation.**

...that I have greatly sinned: The addition of the word "greatly" is accurate and just. It is a paradox of the Christian life that the closer we draw to God, the more keenly we are aware of the terrible offense of sin. We wish to sharpen that awareness, just as we wish to whet our longing for God's transforming love.

...through my fault, through my fault,/ through my most grievous fault: We utter the humbling truth three times, as each of our sins is a rejection of the love of the Holy Trinity. Our prayer here prepares us soon to beg, three times, for God's mercy. We may hear the words of Pontius Pilate, which do not befit us sinners, but do befit the Lord who died for us: "I find in him no fault at all" (Jn 18: 38, KJV).

Have mercy on us, O Lord./ For we have sinned against you: Exactly as in the Latin. We the people complete the thought and the prayer that the priest begins, as if he and we form two parts of a single choir. We humble ourselves before God, because only they who know they are wounded will plead for the Physician: "I said, LORD, be merciful unto me: heal my soul; for I have sinned against thee" (Ps 41: 4, KJV).

• FORM C •

■ You were sent to heal the contrite of heart:
Lord, have mercy.   or: Kyrie, eleison.
■ ■ **Lord, have mercy.**   or: **Kyrie, eleison.**

■ You came to call sinners:
Christ, have mercy.   or: Christe, eleison.
■ ■ **Christ, have mercy.**   or: **Christe, eleison.**

■ You are seated at the right hand of the Father
to intercede for us:
Lord, have mercy.   or: Kyrie, eleison.
■ ■ **Lord, have mercy.**   or: **Kyrie, eleison.**

■ May almighty God have mercy on us,
forgive us our sins,
and bring us to everlasting life.
■ ■ **Amen.**

The Kyrie, eleison (Lord, have mercy) invocations follow, unless they have just occurred in a formula of the Penitential Act.

■ Lord, have mercy.   ■ ■ **Lord, have mercy.**
■ Christ, have mercy.   ■ ■ **Christ, have mercy.**
■ Lord, have mercy.   ■ ■ **Lord, have mercy.**

You were sent to heal the contrite of heart: The final phrase echoes again the *Miserere*, wherein the Psalmist cries out that his heart has been afflicted: "My sacrifice, O God, is a contrite spirit;/ a heart contrite and humbled, O God, you will not spurn" (Ps 51: 19). Just as David knew that God wanted not slain offerings but the holocaust of the heart, so now, as we prepare to celebrate the mystery of Christ's sacrifice of love, we too bring to the altar "a heart contrite and humbled." It is to stress that our sorrow for sin must emerge from the center of our being. So says Jesus (citing Dt 6: 5): "You shall love the Lord your God with all your heart, with all your soul, with all your mind, and with all your strength" (Mk 12: 30).

You are seated at the right hand of the Father to intercede for us: An echo of both the Gloria and the Creed to come, linking the three prayers. Jesus is seated at the right hand of the Father, not simply because he has been raised to glory, but so that we might have the great high priest in that temple not made by human hands, interceding with the Father on our behalf. He is a priest for ever, and "therefore, he is always able to save those who approach God through him, since he lives forever to make intercession for them" (Heb 7: 25). It is a fulfillment of the vision of the Psalmist: "The LORD said to my Lord: Sit at my right hand till/ I make your enemies your footstool" (Ps 110: 1), and declared by Jesus to the chief priests and the elders who put him to death: "From now on you will see 'the Son of Man/ seated at the right hand of the Power'" (Mt 26: 64).

Then, when it is prescribed, this hymn is either sung or said:

GLORY TO GOD in the highest,
and on earth peace to people of good will.

We praise you,
we bless you,
we adore you,
we glorify you,

we give you thanks for your great glory,
Lord God, heavenly King,
O God, almighty Father.

...and on earth peace to people of good will: As in the Latin, we repeat here the song of the angels at the nativity of Christ (Lk 2: 14). The song is like a verse of the Hebrew psalms, with a wise balancing of ideas: we give glory to God in the highest heavens, and we pray on earth for peace to people of good will. We are reminded that it rests in our freely given love whether we shall belong to God, and enjoy even on earth a measure of his peace that passes understanding.

We praise you,/ we bless you,/ we adore you,/ we glorify you: The spilling of verbs is like water flowing over the sides of a fountain. We exult in a multitude of ways of expressing our love for God. We acknowledge his greatness in our praise, we proclaim his holiness in our blessing. We adore him, meaning, literally, we seek his face, we long to look upon him with awe. We glorify him, that is, we rejoice in the radiance of his beauty: "Let them praise the name of the LORD,/ for his name alone is exalted;/ his glory is above earth and heaven" (Ps 148: 13, RSV).

...we give you thanks for your great glory: We do not simply give God thanks, but we thank him for his glory. That touches upon a mystery of love. We do more than say that God is glorious. We revel in his glory. We see that the glory of God is a great gift to us, because he has made us to enjoy that glory, as one delights to behold what is most beautiful and holy.

Lord Jesus Christ, Only Begotten Son,
Lord God, Lamb of God, Son of the Father,

Lord Jesus Christ, Only Begotten Son: An exact translation, meant to echo the Psalmist, foretelling the coming of the Messiah: "You are my son;/ this day I have begotten you" (Ps 2: 7), and the prologue of John's Gospel: "And we beheld his glory, the glory as of the only begotten of the Father" (Jn 1: 14, KJV). Jesus is not *created* by the Father, but *begotten*, the word expressing the eternal relation between the Son and the Father. We hear in Genesis of the many sons begotten of Adam and of Adam's sons in turn; but our begetting of children in time, children who like us come to be and return to the dust, is but a shadow of the eternal begetting of the Son by the Father.

you take away the sins of the world,
>have mercy on us;
you take away the sins of the world,
>receive our prayer;
you are seated at the right hand of the Father,
>have mercy on us.

For you alone are the Holy One,
you alone are the Lord,
you alone are the Most High,
Jesus Christ,
with the Holy Spirit,
in the glory of God the Father. Amen.

■ Let us pray.

> *Then the Priest says the Collect prayer,*
> *at the end of which the people acclaim:*

■■ Amen.

...you take away the sins of the world: The words of John the Baptist: "Behold, the Lamb of God, who takes away the sin of the world" (Jn 1: 29). Jesus, the Lamb of God, takes away our sins by sacrificing himself for us, the innocent for the guilty, God for man, and thus shows us in reality what it is to be like God: "Worthy is the Lamb that was slain/ to receive power and riches, wisdom and strength,/ honor and glory and blessing" (Rv 5: 12). The new translation faithfully follows the order of the original prayer. We address Jesus three times, not twice, again reflecting that our prayer is to the Trinity, and preparing ourselves for the prayer before communion, the *Agnus Dei,* wherein we will also address the Lord three times. Repetition, a prime feature of folk poetry, can stir delight and rouse the mind to contemplation: Jesus gives us a tremendous example of it in the Beatitudes (Mt 5: 3-12), as does the Psalmist in the song the Church sings at Easter (Ps 118: 1-4). The words "receive our prayer" are placed between two utterances of "have mercy on us," since our prayer must begin and end with an appeal to God's freely given grace. He is the one who begins our salvation, and who brings it to completion.

THE LITURGY OF THE WORD

To indicate the end of the readings, the reader acclaims:

■ The word of the Lord.
■ ■ Thanks be to God.

——— • PROCLAMATION OF THE GOSPEL • ———

After this, the Deacon who is to proclaim the Gospel,
bowing profoundly before the Priest, asks for the blessing,
saying in a low voice:

Your blessing, Father.

The Priest says in a low voice:

May the Lord be in your heart and on your lips,
that you may proclaim his Gospel worthily and well,
in the name of the Father, and of the Son, ✠ and of
the Holy Spirit.

The Deacon signs himself with the Sign of the Cross and replies:

Amen.

If, however, a Deacon is not present, the Priest,
bowing before the altar, says quietly:

Cleanse my heart and my lips, almighty God,
that I may worthily proclaim your holy Gospel.

...*worthily and well:* If there is a deacon, he begs the blessing of the priest in these short words: "Your blessing, Father." The priest's reply is slightly changed. He prays that the deacon may proclaim the Gospel "worthily and well, in the name of the Father, and of the Son, and of the Holy Spirit," signing him with the sign of the cross. The addition of the words "and well," following the Latin, expands the import of the prayer, so that we beg the Lord that the proclamation will not only be worthy of the holiness of the Gospel, but that it will be to good effect among those who hear it. It is also significant that the blessing that follows not be separated by a full break from the content of the prayer before. The comma – so slight a change here – links the blessing both to the prayer of the priest *and to the proclamation of the Gospel* by the deacon, so that he too, in reading the Word of God, will do so "in the name of the Father, and of the Son, and of the Holy Spirit."

...*your holy Gospel:* If there is no deacon, the priest prays that God will cleanse his heart and lips that he "may worthily proclaim your holy Gospel." That word of simple and profound truth has been restored. The Gospel would not be good news at all were it not *holy*, that is, something in its own right to be revered, and to be approached with awe and love.

■ The Lord be with you.
■ ■ And with your spirit.

■ A reading from the holy Gospel according to N.
■ ■ Glory to you, O Lord.

At the end of the Gospel, the Deacon, or the Priest, acclaims:

■ The Gospel of the Lord.
■ ■ Praise to you, Lord Jesus Christ.

Then he kisses the book, saying quietly:

Through the words of the Gospel
may our sins be wiped away.

*At the end of the Homily, the Symbol or Profession of Faith or Creed,
when prescribed, is either sung or said.*

Through the words of the Gospel/ may our sins be wiped away: Once the Gospel has been read and the people have acclaimed their praise of Jesus Christ, the priest says quietly, "Through the words of the Gospel may our sins be wiped away." The passive voice here is an exact rendering of the Latin. It is not the words of the Gospel alone and of themselves that wipe away our sins. For many people will hear the Word and remain unmoved, like those who have ears to hear but do not hear. Instead, the Gospel is to be the *means* by which God wipes away our sins; the initiative is God's, and the Gospel is the holy instrument. Again the words echo the *Miserere*: "Turn away your face from my sins;/ blot out all my guilt" (Ps 51: 11).

I BELIEVE IN ONE GOD,
the Father almighty,
maker of heaven and earth,

of all things visible and invisible.

I believe in one God: An exact translation of the Latin *credo*. We are each of us baptized into a community of believers, but we receive the sacrament in our own persons, one by one. When we pray the Creed, then, we place ourselves again at the baptismal font. It is therefore not enough to declare what Christians in general believe, but what *I believe*, that to which I give the assent of my heart and mind and soul.

...of all things visible and invisible: The words "visible and invisible" replace "seen and unseen." The point is not that God makes things we happen to see and things we happen not to see, but things that can be seen, like all the beauties of earth and the spangled stars in the sky, and things that by their very nature cannot be seen. Those include the spiritual beings we call angels, the messengers of God whom we can see only if they manifest themselves to us, and such non-material things as the moral law. So when we utter these words, we proclaim the truth that what can be seen by man is but a portion, indeed quite a small portion, of all that is. The words echo those of an ancient hymn to Christ, preserved for us by Saint Paul: "He is the image of the invisible God,/ the firstborn of all creation./ For in him were created all things in heaven and on earth,/ the visible and the invisible,/ whether thrones or dominions or principalities or powers;/ all things were created through him and for him" (Col 1: 15-16). Thus too the verse, accurately rendered, helps to join our praise of the Father with our praise of the Son which follows, "through him all things were made."

I believe in one Lord Jesus Christ,
the Only Begotten Son of God,
born of the Father before all ages.

God from God, Light from Light,
true God from true God,
begotten, not made, consubstantial with the Father;
through him all things were made.

...the Only Begotten Son of God,/ born of the Father before all ages: Christ is eternally begotten of the Father, and here the idea is given a precise and yet poetic form: *before all ages.* We may think of the birth of Jesus in the fullness of time, as a man to dwell among us. But before that time, even before there was such a thing as time at all, Christ is begotten and born of the Father. That is not something that happened, in the way that an event happens on earth. There was never the Father without the Son and the Holy Spirit. All things and all times, from the beginning to the end of the world, are the creation of the Blessed Trinity. "He is before all things," says Saint Paul (Col 1: 17). "I am the first and the last," says Christ in the Book of Revelation, "the one who lives" (Rv 1: 17-18).

...consubstantial with the Father: Christ is not simply one with the Father, as two separate beings joined together in love. The Father, the Son, and the Spirit share the same *substance* or essence. The word "substance" here is used with its ancient philosophical meaning: it does not signify the matter that composes a thing (for God is not a lowly mass of created matter, like the earth), but rather the essence that makes a thing the sort of thing it is. Since God is One, if Christ is *consubstantial* with the Father, then he too is God, and not a different God, but the same. That explains Jesus' response to the Apostle Philip, who asked him to show them the Father. "Have I been with you for so long a time," says Jesus, "and you still do not know me, Philip? Whoever has seen me has

For us men and for our salvation
he came down from heaven,

At the words that follow, up to and including and became man,
all bow.

and by the Holy Spirit was incarnate of the Virgin Mary,
and became man.

For our sake he was crucified under Pontius Pilate,
he suffered death and was buried,
and rose again on the third day
in accordance with the Scriptures.
He ascended into heaven
and is seated at the right hand of the Father.
He will come again in glory
to judge the living and the dead
and his kingdom will have no end.

I believe in the Holy Spirit, the Lord, the giver of life,
who proceeds from the Father and the Son,
who with the Father and the Son is adored
  and glorified,
who has spoken through the prophets.

seen the Father… Do you not believe that I am in the Father and the Father is in me?" (Jn 14: 9-10). So also the Holy Spirit. Father, Son, and Spirit are not one *in* or *by means* of being, but One Being, three Persons in one Being. Again we are invited to dwell more fully upon the highest mystery of love, which is that communion of Persons in the Holy Trinity.

…was incarnate of the Virgin Mary: Yes, Jesus was born of the Virgin Mary, but nine months before he was born, he the eternal Word became flesh, and dwelt among us. That happened at the Annunciation, when Mary replied to the angel, "Behold, I am the handmaid of the Lord. May it be done to me according to your word" (Lk 1: 38). We meditate here upon that enfleshment, that incarnation, the sudden breaking of God's grace through the walls of our sinful world. He does so quietly, in a room with no one present but Mary and his messenger, and when Mary utters those words of humility, the wonder is accomplished, and God has taken on our human nature, our *flesh*, in both its beauty and its infirmity. We have then a Savior who knows our sufferings in the flesh: "In the days when he was in the flesh, he offered prayers and supplications with loud cries and tears to the one who was able to save him from death" (Heb 5: 7).

I believe in one, holy, catholic and apostolic Church.
I confess one Baptism for the forgiveness of sins

and I look forward to the resurrection of the dead
and the life of the world to come.
Amen.

I confess one Baptism: To *confess* is to do more than *acknowledge* or admit. It is to proclaim, to declare publicly. We must be bold in our proclamation. Jesus himself says, "I am the way and the truth and the life. No one comes to the Father except through me" (Jn 14: 6). Everyone who is saved is saved by Jesus. Everyone who is baptized into his death, and who does not betray that sacred bond, will be raised by him to newness of life: "If you confess with your mouth that Jesus is Lord and believe in your heart that God raised him from the dead, you will be saved" (Rom 10: 9). That the baptism is *one* follows from the oneness of God, and is meant to bind us into one body, confessing "one Lord, one faith, one baptism; one God and Father of all, who is over all and through all and in all" (Eph 4: 5-6).

...and I look forward to the resurrection of the dead: We await it with yearning. Recall, in Luke's Gospel, the aged prophet Simeon who goes to the temple to pray, who is awaiting or looking forward to the consolation of Israel. He is confident in its coming. He has received the promise of God that he will witness it, and so he does, when Mary and Joseph present the child Jesus at the temple. We too should live in that bold expectation, saying with the Apostle John, "Beloved, we are God's children now; what we shall be has not yet been revealed. We do know that when it is revealed we shall be like him, for we shall see him as he is" (1 Jn 3: 2).

*Instead of the Niceno-Constantinopolitan Creed, especially during Lent
and Easter Time, the baptismal Symbol of the Roman Church, known
as the Apostles' Creed, may be used.*

I BELIEVE IN GOD,
the Father almighty,
Creator of heaven and earth,
and in Jesus Christ, his only Son, our Lord,

> *At the words that follow, up to and including* the Virgin Mary,
> *all bow.*

who was conceived by the Holy Spirit,
born of the Virgin Mary,
suffered under Pontius Pilate,
was crucified, died and was buried;
he descended into hell;
on the third day he rose again from the dead;
he ascended into heaven,
and is seated at the right hand of God the Father
   almighty;
from there he will come to judge the living and the dead.

I believe in the Holy Spirit,
the holy catholic Church,
the communion of saints,
the forgiveness of sins,
the resurrection of the body,
and life everlasting.
Amen.

...*he descended into hell:* Literally, the regions below. It is not simply that Jesus died. He took the realm of death by storm. Hell is that place where men of their free choice have turned toward death rather than life, setting themselves up as gods, and severing themselves from friendship with God, the giver of life and of all good things. Jesus descended, then, into the deepest abyss of our sin, which is but the yawning gulf of death, to set souls free from bondage to sin and death. He takes captivity captive, as Saint Paul says, for "he also descended into the lower [regions] of the earth" (Eph 4: 9), and, as the Church teaches, he brings the souls of those who awaited his coming to the freedom of eternal life. It is the completion of his having descended from heaven to dwell among us.

THE LITURGY OF THE EUCHARIST

■ Blessed are you, Lord God of all creation,
for through your goodness we have received
the bread we offer you:

fruit of the earth and work of human hands,
it will become for us the bread of life.

■■ Blessed be God for ever.

...the bread we offer you: The indirect object of "offer" has been restored, here and in the prayer offering the wine. People do not simply *offer* things; an offering is given by a person to a person. The restored pronoun emphasizes the personal relationship embodied in the offering. God gives us his gifts, and from them we fashion a gift to return to him in gratitude. It is intriguing to consider that there is a veiled promise in the judgment that God pronounces against the sinful Adam, "By the sweat of your face/ shall you get bread to eat" (Gn 3: 19). It is the first appearance of the word "bread" in Scripture, and looks forward not only to the manna showered down upon the Israelites in the desert, but to the true manna, born in the flesh in a small village called *Beth-lehem*, "House of Bread," and who offers himself to the Father on our behalf, and to us in the Eucharist: "I am the bread of life," says Jesus (Jn 6: 35).

...fruit of the earth and work of human hands: When God made the heavens and the earth, he blessed the living things he had made, saying, "Be fruitful and multiply" (Gn 1: 22, RSV). Then when he made man in his image, he gave him the same blessing, and added, "Fill the earth and subdue it" (Gn 1: 28), granting to him what was to be a loving dominion over all of the physical creation. In other words, man was given the nobility of work, to share in God's power by his own freedom and skill and love. Those blessings were compromised by sin, but not swept aside completely. When the children of Israel were to enter the Promised Land, they were

■ Blessed are you, Lord God of all creation,
for through your goodness we have received
the wine we offer you:
fruit of the vine and work of human hands,
it will become our spiritual drink.
■ ■ **Blessed be God for ever.**

■ Pray, brethren (brothers and sisters),
that my sacrifice and yours
may be acceptable to God,
the almighty Father.

The people rise and reply:

■ ■ **May the Lord accept the sacrifice at your hands**
for the praise and glory of his name,
for our good
and the good of all his holy Church.

Then the Priest says the Prayer over the Offerings,
at the end of which the people acclaim:

■ ■ **Amen.**

instructed to take from the first fruits of the land where they had settled and offer them to the Lord (Dt 26: 2). So even in our Eucharist, the bread that raises us up to the true homeland, God asks us to unite the natural fruits of the earth with our own labor, for he aims to redeem us, and through us, the whole of creation.

...that my sacrifice and yours: There is a subtle difference between saying "mine and yours" and "ours." When we say "ours," we make no distinction among persons or groups. But there is a distinction to be made here, and a great truth to proclaim. The priest is not simply one of us, but the man whom God has chosen to offer the sacrifice on our behalf. That is what he means when he calls it *my sacrifice*. Then he says it is also *ours*. For we too are priests of God, a holy people, a nation set apart.

...his holy Church: There is no need to omit the word "holy." We know that the Church on earth is made up of sinners. How could it be otherwise? How could it be the ship of our salvation, if sinners could not be admitted aboard? Yet this same Church has been sanctified by the blood of Jesus. If he looks upon it with love and takes it to him as a bridegroom takes his bride, let us then never deny the holiness of that Bride, but rather pray that he may make us also holy, and without spot. For Christ has handed himself over to die, to sanctify the Church, "that he might present to himself the church in splendor, without spot or wrinkle or any such thing, that she might be holy and without blemish" (Eph 5: 27).

• THE PREFACE •

■ The Lord be with you.
■■ **And with your spirit.**
■ Lift up your hearts.
■■ **We lift them up to the Lord.**
■ Let us give thanks to the Lord our God.
■■ **It is right and just.**

The Priest continues the Preface.
At the end he concludes with the people:

Holy, Holy, Holy Lord God of hosts.
Heaven and earth are full of your glory.
Hosanna in the highest.
Blessed is he who comes in the name of the Lord.
Hosanna in the highest.

It is right and just: The translation is brief, as the Latin itself is. First we affirm that it is the *right* or worthy thing to do, to thank God, and then we affirm that it is also *just*. For a thing may be right in many ways. If I am ill, it is right for me to beg God for healing, since it is correct for me to acknowledge his power and virtuous for me to trust in him. Yet if I did not beg for healing – if instead I prayed for the healing of others – I would not necessarily be committing a wrong. But our thanks to God is right because it is *just*: we owe him that debt of gratitude.

Lord God of hosts: Perhaps the most common phrase to describe the Lord, heard by the prophet Isaiah in his great vision in the temple, and echoed here in our prayer: "Holy, holy, holy is the LORD of hosts" (Is 6: 3). The words here show that God makes his power manifest in a special way through the hosts of angels who attend him. When he made the world, as we read in the Book of Job, "all the sons of God shouted for joy" (Jb 38: 7). These are the angels who minister about his altar, or who guard us in our weakness, or who fight on our behalf. They and the saints are one in the Church triumphant, against whose onslaught, says Jesus, the gates of hell shall not prevail (Mt 16: 18).

Eucharistic Prayer I
(The Roman Canon)

To you, therefore, most merciful Father,
we make humble prayer and petition
through Jesus Christ, your Son, our Lord:

that you accept
and bless ✠ these gifts, these offerings,
these holy and unblemished sacrifices,
which we offer you firstly
for your holy catholic Church.

To you, therefore: The Latin takes care to link one prayer with the next, for what we say now is consequent upon what we have said before. It is *because* Christ has come to us *in the name of the Lord* that now we too, through Christ, approach the Father in prayer.

…most merciful Father: God looks upon us with kindness and clemency, despite our sins.

…we make humble prayer and petition: Literally, we bend the knee before you and beg you to hear our plea. It is good for us to do so, for "God opposes the proud/ but bestows favor on the humble" (1 Pt 5: 5). Man never stands so tall as when he is on his knees.

…these gifts, these offerings,/ these holy and unblemished sacrifices: Exactly as in the Latin. The sequence of nouns builds to a climax. A *gift* may be given by one person to another; an *offering* is given to one's superior; a sacrifice, only to God. But these *sacrifices* are holy and unblemished, because they are the Lord's own gift of himself, the unblemished Passover Lamb of God.

Be pleased to grant her peace,
to guard, unite and govern her
throughout the whole world,
together with your servant N. our Pope
and N. our Bishop,
and all those who, holding to the truth,
hand on the catholic and apostolic faith.

Commemoration of the Living

REMEMBER, Lord, your servants N. and N.
and all gathered here,
whose faith and devotion are known to you.
For them, we offer you this sacrifice of praise
or they offer it for themselves
and all who are dear to them:
for the redemption of their souls,
in hope of health and well-being,
and paying their homage to you,
the eternal God, living and true.

Be pleased to grant her peace: We wish for more than a kind of truce, or absence of strife. We wish for the favor of God, in whose will alone we find our peace, for God himself is "the Lord of peace" (2 Thes 3: 16), and "he is our peace" (Eph 2: 14). Therefore we beg that God will *be pleased* to grant peace to us, his Church, taking us under his loving wing.

…govern her/ throughout the whole world: The phrase "throughout the whole world" has been reunited with its verb. We do pray that the Church may be made one. But we complete our prayer by begging that God will be the one who governs her wherever she may be found.

…your servant: The phrase has been restored. The pope is our guide on earth because he is a *servant* of God, literally a member of his household.

…or they offer it for themselves: Here and continuing through to the end of the sentence, the priest suggests that the souls of the departed may be joining us in the Eucharistic sacrifice, beseeching God both for themselves and for those whom they loved on earth. "We are surrounded," says the author of the Letter to the Hebrews, "by so great a cloud of witnesses" (Heb 12: 1). The souls of our beloved dead, who fell asleep in the hope of Christ, do not abandon us. The Church teaches us that they are with us still. We pray for them, yes, but they too pray for themselves and for us, in the confident hope that we will all be one again in the kingdom of God.

Within the Action.

IN COMMUNION with those whose memory we venerate,
especially the glorious ever-Virgin Mary,
Mother of our God and Lord, Jesus Christ,
and blessed Joseph, her Spouse,
your blessed Apostles and Martyrs,
Peter and Paul, Andrew,
(James, John,
Thomas, James, Philip,
Bartholomew, Matthew,
Simon and Jude;
Linus, Cletus, Clement, Sixtus,
Cornelius, Cyprian,
Lawrence, Chrysogonus,
John and Paul,
Cosmas and Damian)
and all your Saints;
we ask that through their merits and prayers,
in all things we may be defended
by your protecting help.
(Through Christ our Lord. Amen.)

In communion with those whose memory we venerate: We are encouraged to give due honor to the souls of those who have gone before us in faith. We should remember them, for they are a gift of God to us, showing us how many are the ways of God's saving grace in human lives.

…especially the glorious ever-Virgin Mary: When we think of the saints, we should meditate first and most devotedly upon Mary, upon her whose face indeed most closely resembles the face of Christ. She partakes of his glory more fully than does any other created being, even the cherubim and the seraphim.

…and blessed Joseph, her Spouse: Joseph is *blessed* by God not simply to be the husband of Mary, but to be her *Spouse*, literally, the man who responds with a promise to a promise, to be her true protector until death. The word helps us to see in Joseph, the foster-father of Jesus, an image of Christ the Spouse of the Church, and indeed we venerate Saint Joseph as the Church's patron and protector.

…your blessed Apostles and Martyrs: They are blessed because they are yours, O Lord.

THEREFORE, Lord, we pray:
graciously accept this oblation of our service,
that of your whole family;

order our days in your peace,

and command that we be delivered from eternal
   damnation

and counted among the flock of those you have
   chosen.
(Through Christ our Lord. Amen.)

...graciously accept this oblation of our service: It is more than a bare offering. It is an offering to God, an *oblation*, of our service, our willingness to obey the Lord in all things, and particularly in his command that we celebrate the Eucharist. We ask God to accept the offering *graciously*, that, literally, he will be pleased to accept it, because what we truly seek is his favor and love.

...order our days in your peace: We ask here for more than peace among nations. We ask that our days might be *ordered* in the peace of God; and that means that we beg to be governed by God's will, wherein we find our peace. The language is that of the Psalmist: "Order my steps in thy word: and let not any iniquity have dominion over me" (Ps 119: 133, KJV).

...and command that we be delivered from eternal damnation: Literally, that we might be snatched as if from the jaws of hell. The verb "delivered" reminds us that evil is a prison from which we long to be set free. The word also echoes Jesus in the Lord's Prayer, and a host of pleas and thanksgivings in the Psalms, the prophets, and the letters of Saint Paul: "You have delivered my soul from death,/ my eyes from tears,/ and my feet from stumbling" (Ps 116: 8, RSV).

...and counted among the flock of those you have chosen: In the Old Testament, the prophets commonly refer to the children of Israel as God's chosen *flock*: "Like a shepherd he feeds his flock;/ in his arms he gathers the lambs" (Is 40: 11). Indeed, the Latin word we use to describe the people of a

Be pleased, O God, we pray,
to bless, acknowledge,
and approve this offering in every respect;
make it spiritual and acceptable,
so that it may become for us

the Body and Blood of your most beloved Son,
our Lord Jesus Christ.

local church, the *congregation*, literally means the gathering of a *flock*. The image reminds us that Jesus saves us by taking us among his flock: "There will be one flock, one shepherd" (Jn 10: 16).

...*make it spiritual and acceptable:* Echoing the words of Jesus, that his words, commanding us to eat his flesh and drink his blood, are "spirit and life" (Jn 6: 63). The point is not that we make this offering in a good spirit, but that we beg God to transform this offering, one of bread and wine, into the genuinely *spiritual* and therefore *acceptable* offering of Christ himself. Then we ourselves will be transformed: "Let yourselves be built into a spiritual house to be a holy priest-hood to offer spiritual sacrifices acceptable to God through Jesus Christ" (1 Pt 2: 5).

...*your most beloved Son:* We hear an echo of the words of the Father, when Jesus went to the Jordan to be baptized by John: "This is my beloved Son, with whom I am well pleased" (Mt 3: 17).

ON THE DAY before he was to suffer,
he took bread in his holy and venerable hands,

and with eyes raised to heaven

to you, O God, his almighty Father,
giving you thanks, he said the blessing,
broke the bread
and gave it to his disciples, saying:

> TAKE THIS, ALL OF YOU, AND EAT OF IT,
> FOR THIS IS MY BODY,
> WHICH WILL BE GIVEN UP FOR YOU.

...he took bread in his holy and venerable hands: Because they are holy, they are deserving of our most profound veneration. The sentence suggests more than a statement of fact, "He took bread." We behold the *hands*, hands that Jesus had stretched out in blessing, hands that touched the lame and the blind and healed them, and hands that would soon be pierced for our offenses. The words of the institution of the Blessed Sacrament are to be found in several places in the New Testament, in slightly different forms (Mt 26: 26-29; Mk 14: 22-25; Lk 22: 14-20; 1 Cor 11: 23-26).

...and with eyes raised to heaven: Bold and clear. We see Jesus before us, raising his eyes, as he did when he prayed that Lazarus would rise from the grave (Jn 11: 41). The penitent publican in Jesus' parable would not so much as raise his eyes to heaven (Lk 18: 13), but perhaps we, uniting ourselves with Jesus, may now have the audacity to do so.

...he said the blessing: As Jews would do before any meal. This too is meant as a guide for us.

IN A SIMILAR WAY, when supper was ended,
he took this precious chalice
in his holy and venerable hands,
and once more giving you thanks, he said the blessing
and gave the chalice to his disciples, saying:

> TAKE THIS, ALL OF YOU, AND DRINK FROM IT,
> FOR THIS IS THE CHALICE OF MY BLOOD,
> THE BLOOD OF THE NEW AND ETERNAL COVENANT,
>
> WHICH WILL BE POURED OUT FOR YOU
>   AND FOR MANY
> FOR THE FORGIVENESS OF SINS.
>
> DO THIS IN MEMORY OF ME.

Not all will accept Jesus
salvation!

In a similar way: The text binds together the blessing of the bread with the blessing of the wine.

…he took this precious chalice: It is not, now, an ordinary cup. Jesus was celebrating the great feast of the Passover, and inaugurating the fulfillment of that feast, in the Eucharist. The cup has been sanctified, and is no longer for mere earthly use.

…the new and eternal covenant: The word "eternal" means all that everlasting means, and more. It suggests not only that this covenant will never end. It suggests that this covenant has for ever been the key of God's plan for mankind. We are invited to join the wedding feast that is God's love, beyond the bounds of time. So the Father, in the words of the prophet, promises us "rich fare" that brings life, as in the Eucharist he renews "the everlasting covenant,/ the benefits assured to David" (Is 55: 3).

…which will be poured out for you and for many: The words of Jesus: "This is my blood of the covenant, which will be shed on behalf of many for the forgiveness of sins" (Mt 26: 28). Jesus is too generous merely to shed his blood for us. He *pours* it out, like a lavish offering of wine. We too are encouraged to follow the example of Christ, as when Saint Paul, at the end of his life, writes, "I am already being poured out like a libation" (2 Tm 4: 6). The words "for many" translate, exactly, the Latin *pro multis*. They do not imply that Jesus wished to save only a few. For as Saint Paul says, he would have all men to be saved (1 Tm 2: 4). But not all will accept this salvation.

■ The mystery of faith.

■■ We proclaim your Death, O Lord,
and profess your Resurrection
until you come again.

Or:

■■ When we eat this Bread and drink this Cup,
we proclaim your Death, O Lord,
until you come again.

The mystery of faith: The Latin is abrupt and powerful *(Mysterium fidei)*. It refers not to our reply to the priest's words, but to what has just transpired. The Word, through whom all things were made, those visible and invisible, has become present in his full reality under the appearances of bread and wine. This miracle of love fulfills, in a most intimate way, Jesus' promise to his disciples after the Resurrection, when he said, "Behold, I am with you always, until the end of the age" (Mt 28: 20).

We proclaim your Death, O Lord,/ and profess your Resurrection: Our response to the priest's proclamation is a meditation upon the meaning of the Eucharist as we go forth in the Christian life. When we partake of the Sacrament, we do not merely engage in a pious memorial. By our actions we profess the death and Resurrection of Christ, rejoicing that the body that was broken has been raised again, and praying that we too will be found worthy to be members of his mystical body, the Church.

When we eat this Bread and drink this Cup: The words of Saint Paul, after he has recalled the words of our Lord at the Last Supper: "For as often as you eat this bread and drink the cup, you proclaim the death of the Lord until he comes" (1 Cor 11: 26). The death of Jesus on the cross is thus inseparable from the Blessed Sacrament, because he gives us of himself utterly, to the end, nourishing us with this broken bread, the bread of life, that we might die with him and also rise with him.

Or:

■ ■ Save us, Savior of the world,
for by your Cross and Resurrection
you have set us free.

THEREFORE, O Lord,
as we celebrate the memorial
  of the blessed Passion,
the Resurrection from the dead,
and the glorious Ascension into heaven
of Christ, your Son, our Lord,
we, your servants and your holy people,
offer to your glorious majesty
from the gifts that you have given us,
this pure victim,
this holy victim,
this spotless victim,

Save us, Savior of the world: The yearning appeal, in Latin *salva nos*, has been restored. The words recall the cry of the disciples in the midst of the storm on the Sea of Galilee: "Lord, save us! We are perishing" (Mt 8: 25). The cross and Resurrection of the Lord have *set us free* from the storms of sin and the death impending, and we and all creation look forward to "the glorious freedom of the children of God" (Rom 8: 21).

Therefore, O Lord: We have not ceased to meditate upon the great gift of the Blessed Sacrament. It is not simply a matter of recalling. We wish to place ourselves too in the presence of the Lord. It is because of that gift that we now celebrate the memorial of the blessed Passion, the Resurrection, and the glorious Ascension of our Lord into heaven.

...this pure victim,/ this holy victim,/ this spotless victim: Again the poetry of the prayer brings to our minds the Trinity, for it is the Father who accepts the sacrifice of the Son by the ministry of their Spirit of love. Jesus is the Lamb of God, the Passover victim who is pure, holy, and without spot. We are redeemed, says Saint Peter, not by things that perish like silver and gold, but by "the precious blood of Christ as of a spotless unblemished lamb" (1 Pt 1: 19).

the holy Bread of eternal life
and the Chalice of everlasting salvation.

Be pleased to look upon these offerings
with a serene and kindly countenance,
and to accept them,

as once you were pleased to accept
the gifts of your servant Abel the just,
the sacrifice of Abraham, our father in faith,

...the holy Bread of eternal life: Exactly as in the Latin. We must not forget that the Bread is now *holy*, made so by the wondrous grace of God. Common bread is "the staff of life," but this Bread is more than a prop or a support. It is itself a communication of the life of God. As Saint Thomas Aquinas says, we do not assimilate the Eucharist to ourselves, but through the Blessed Sacrament God assimilates us to him.

...with a serene and kindly countenance: The ancient Hebrews were forbidden to make any graven images of God. Such images would undoubtedly have caused them to imagine God to be like us, only greater and immortal. Yet the Psalmist still speaks of his yearning to see the face of God: "One thing I ask of the LORD; this I seek:/ To dwell in the house of the LORD all the days of my life,/ That I may gaze on the loveliness of the LORD and contemplate his temple" (Ps 27: 4). That is because God is a Person – and we, with our capacity to know and to love, are made in his image. So it is mysteriously fitting that the Hebrews, even before the coming of the Messiah in the flesh, should pray that God might make his face to shine upon them (Nm 6: 25).

...your servant Abel the just: The prayer moves to a climax, from Abel to Abraham to Melchizedek. Abel is a foreshadowing of Jesus, put to death by the envy of the wicked. His blood cried out to the Lord for vengeance, but the blood of Christ "speaks more eloquently than that of Abel" (Heb 12: 24). His sacrifice met with favor in God's eyes, because it came from the fullness of his heart.

and the offering of your high priest Melchizedek,
a holy sacrifice, a spotless victim.

IN HUMBLE PRAYER we ask you, almighty God:

command that these gifts be borne
by the hands of your holy Angel
to your altar on high

in the sight of your divine majesty,

...your high priest Melchizedek: The name of this mysterious worshiper of God who blessed Abraham by offering bread and wine to God means "righteous king," and thus it is a kind of allusion to God himself. He is not just any priest, but the *high* priest, and so he too foreshadows the great high priest, Christ, who offers himself, a holy sacrifice, a spotless victim. We now have a high priest who has penetrated the veil of the everlasting temple: Jesus, who is "high priest forever according to the order of Melchizedek" (Heb 6: 20).

In humble prayer: We should ever remember to try to practice the difficult virtue of humility, especially as we kneel in the presence of God, for as the Lord himself says, "He who humbles himself will be exalted" (Lk 14: 11, RSV), and, "Learn from me, for I am meek and humble of heart" (Mt 11: 29).

...borne/ by the hands of your holy Angel: "The smoke of the incense along with the prayers of the holy ones went up before God from the hand of the angel" (Rv 8: 4). Again the image is concrete and daring. We know that angels are spiritual beings, but they too labor in joyful obedience to God, and we are encouraged to see them ministering about our altar here, as they do also before God in heaven.

...in the sight of your divine majesty: The gifts we offer are not transferred from one place to another, as by a shuttle. They are brought before the presence of God, where we too long one day to be, to rejoice in the radiance of his kingship. For those who are saved will "lift up their voice in acclaim" and "proclaim the majesty of the Lord" (Is 24: 14).

so that all of us, who through this participation
  at the altar
receive the most holy Body and Blood of your Son,
may be filled with every grace and heavenly blessing.
(Through Christ our Lord. Amen.)

Commemoration of the Dead

REMEMBER also, Lord, your servants N. and N.,
who have gone before us with the sign of faith

and rest in the sleep of peace.
Grant them, O Lord, we pray,
and all who sleep in Christ,

a place of refreshment, light and peace.
(Through Christ our Lord. Amen.)

...*every grace and heavenly blessing:* The words of Saint Paul: "Blessed be the God and Father of our Lord Jesus Christ, who has blessed us in Christ with every spiritual blessing in the heavens" (Eph 1: 3). The blessings of God not only come from heaven, but are themselves an invitation to us to participate more fully, even now, in the life of heaven, as we make our journey there.

Remember also, Lord, your servants: What dignity do we claim, to be servants of God! The good Christian must long to hear, as the crown of his life, the words of the Lord, "Well done, my good and faithful servant!... Come, share your master's joy" (Mt 25: 23).

...*and rest in the sleep of peace:* We recall the words of Saint Paul, who gave consolation to the early Christians, instructing them to think of their beloved dead as having "fallen asleep" in Christ (1 Cor 15: 18).

...*a place of refreshment, light and peace:* As opposed to the ravenous fires below, or the more ravenous fires within the heart of the soul given over to wickedness. We pray for the souls of those who have died in faith, as Saint Peter appealed to the people on Pentecost: "Repent, therefore, and be converted, that your sins may be wiped away, and that the Lord may grant you times of refreshment and send you the

To us, also, your servants, who, though sinners,

hope in your abundant mercies,
graciously grant some share

and fellowship with your holy Apostles and Martyrs:
with John the Baptist, Stephen,
Matthias, Barnabas,
(Ignatius, Alexander,
Marcellinus, Peter,
Felicity, Perpetua,
Agatha, Lucy,
Agnes, Cecilia, Anastasia)
and all your Saints;
admit us, we beseech you,
into their company,

Messiah already appointed for you, Jesus" (Acts 3: 19-20). Recall that Jesus is the good shepherd, who gives his life, his very body, for the sheep. So says the Psalmist: "In verdant pastures he gives me repose;/ Beside restful waters he leads me; he refreshes my soul" (Ps 23: 2-3).

...*though sinners:* We place the word "sinners" at the forefront, because that is what we are. Hear the prayer of the publican in Jesus' parable: "O God, be merciful to me a sinner" (Lk 18: 13).

...*your abundant mercies:* God is not sparing of his gifts, but exuberant and over brimming, like an inexhaustible fountain. "Where sin abounded," says Saint Paul, "grace did much more abound" (Rom 5: 20, KJV).

...*your holy Apostles and Martyrs:* They were sinners like ourselves, but they accepted the grace of God, who made them *holy*, as he wishes to make us likewise.

...*admit us, we beseech you,/ into their company:* For they are now the blessed guests at the wedding feast of the Lamb. We beg for more than an abstract fellowship. We know that the saints are now like Jesus, and thus more human than ever they were on earth. When Jesus rose from the dead, he made sure that his disciples touched his body, spoke to him, even supped with him. The saints in glory likewise look upon one another with joy.

not weighing our merits,
but granting us your pardon,
through Christ our Lord.

THROUGH whom
you continue to make all these good things, O Lord;
you sanctify them, fill them with life,

bless them, and bestow them upon us.

■ Through him, and with him, and in him,
O God, almighty Father,
in the unity of the Holy Spirit,
all glory and honor is yours,
for ever and ever.
■■ Amen.

...*not weighing our merits:* See the fearful words of the prophet Daniel to the Babylonian king: "You have been weighed on the scales and found wanting" (Dn 5: 27). The Latin prayer entreats God not to reckon up our deservings, as if he should find that he owed us anything. We ask instead for God's pardon.

...*you continue to make all these good things:* When does the Creation happen? It is happening now. God the Creator sustains the world in being by his free gift. He is ever the Creator, and here, in this lowly place, he has made mere bread and wine to be the Body and Blood of his Son, our Lord.

...*and bestow them upon us:* God does more than give. He gives abundantly. The Latin suggests that he is utterly free and generous with his gifts; he *bestows* them, as if he meant to endow us with them for ever.

Eucharistic Prayer II

IT IS TRULY right and just, our duty and our
     salvation,
always and everywhere to give you thanks,
  Father most holy,
through your beloved Son, Jesus Christ,
your Word through whom you made all things,
whom you sent as our Savior and Redeemer,
incarnate by the Holy Spirit and born of the Virgin.

Fulfilling your will and gaining for you a holy people,
he stretched out his hands as he endured his Passion,
so as to break the bonds of death and manifest the
   resurrection.

And so, with the Angels and all the Saints
we declare your glory,
as with one voice we acclaim:

HOLY, Holy, Holy Lord God of hosts.
     Heaven and earth are full of your glory.
Hosanna in the highest.
Blessed is he who comes in the name of the Lord.
Hosanna in the highest.

You are indeed Holy, O Lord,
   the fount of all holiness.
Make holy, therefore, these gifts,
   we pray,
by sending down your Spirit upon
   them like the dewfall,
so that they may become for us
the Body and ✠ Blood of our Lord Jesus Christ.

...*like the dewfall:* The image is deeply suggestive. It echoes the image in the previous line, wherein we declare that God is the origin or *fount* of all holiness, abounding in the gift of his holy being. His gifts often come to us quietly, as did the manna to the Israelites in the desert, that first and perishable bread from heaven: "In the morning a dew lay all about the camp," says the sacred author, and when the dew was gone, there were left the fine flakes of manna (Ex 16: 13-14). Here we think of the Holy Spirit, whose work is quiet and secret, but who brings life to the parched soul, as the early morning dewfall on a desert land. So too did the Spirit brood upon the waters at the Creation (Gn 1: 2), and so too did he overshadow the womb of the Virgin Mary.

At the time he was betrayed
and entered willingly into his Passion,
he took bread and, giving thanks, broke it,
and gave it to his disciples, saying:

> Take this, all of you, and eat of it,
> for this is my Body,
> which will be given up for you.

In a similar way, when supper was ended,
he took the chalice
and, once more giving thanks,
he gave it to his disciples, saying:

> Take this, all of you, and drink from it,
> for this is the chalice of my Blood,
> the Blood of the new and eternal covenant,
> which will be poured out for you
>   and for many
> for the forgiveness of sins.
>
> Do this in memory of me.

> *He shows the chalice to the people,*
> *places it on the corporal, and genuflects in adoration.*

At the time he was betrayed/ and entered willingly into his Passion: Literally, Jesus was *handed over*. We recall that Jesus did not simply die for our sins. We *betrayed* God by our sins, and then betrayed the Savior he sent to free us. Consider the contrast between God's loyalty and our betrayal. Then consider the loyalty of Jesus, who sweat blood in the garden of Gethsemane, so intense was his suffering on account of our sins even before he carried the bitter cross; his soul was "sorrowful even to death" (Mk 14: 34). Yet he united his will with the will of the Father, praying, "Father, if you are willing, take this cup away from me; still, not my will but yours be done" (Lk 22: 42). The Passion is the climax of Christ's entering willingly into the infirmities of our nature, for he "emptied himself, taking the form of a servant, being born in the likeness of men," and he "humbled himself and became obedient unto death, even death on a cross" (Phil 2: 7-8, RSV). That is what the Good Shepherd does, laying down his life for the sheep, not by compulsion but *willingly*: "I lay it down of my own accord. I have power to lay it down, and I have power to take it again" (Jn 10: 18, RSV).

■ The mystery of faith.

■■ We proclaim your Death, O Lord,
and profess your Resurrection
until you come again.

Or:

■■ When we eat this Bread and drink this Cup,
we proclaim your Death, O Lord,
until you come again.

Or:

■■ Save us, Savior of the world,
for by your Cross and Resurrection
you have set us free.

THEREFORE, as we celebrate
the memorial of his Death and Resurrection,
we offer you, Lord,
the Bread of life and the Chalice of salvation,
giving thanks that you have held us worthy
to be in your presence and minister to you.

Humbly we pray
that, partaking of the Body and Blood of Christ,
we may be gathered into one by the Holy Spirit.

...*the Bread of life and the Chalice of salvation:* The Bread gives life, and the cup gives salvation, but the language says more than that. The Bread is not only the cause that those who eat of it shall live, but is itself the life of that life, for Jesus says, "I am the bread of life" (Jn 6: 35). He thus associates the power of the bread of the Eucharist with his eternal being. To partake of the Bread of life, then, is to unite oneself with Jesus, the Resurrection and the life.

...*and minister to you:* That is, we serve the Father now as priests, offering to him the sacrifice of his Son, our Lord.

...*partaking of the Body and Blood of Christ:* The structure of the sentence suggests that we pray that God will gather us *into one* by our *partaking* of the Eucharist. That is, the union is not something that happens separately from our sharing of the Eucharist, or after it; the sacrament is essential to our union. We pray, too, not simply that we will possess an abstract quality such as *unity*, but that we will quite literally be gathered as *one*, one flock, one body: "The cup of blessing that we bless, is it not a participation in the blood of Christ? The bread that we break, is it not a participation in the body of Christ? Because the loaf of bread is one, we, though many, are one body, for we all partake of the one loaf" (1 Cor 10: 16-17).

REMEMBER, Lord, your Church,
spread throughout the world,

and bring her to the fullness of charity,
**together with N. our Pope and N. our Bishop
and all the clergy.**

In Masses for the Dead, the following may be added:

REMEMBER your servant N.,
whom you have called (today)
from this world to yourself.

Grant that he (she) who was united with your Son in
  a death like his,
may also be one with him in his Resurrection.

...your Church,/ spread throughout the world: The participle reminds us that our task is an active and generous one, to pour out or spread the Word of God to all nations.

...and bring her to the fullness of charity: We wish to do more than to grow in love. We wish to be *perfected* in love, and the love that we long for is not the natural human affection, but the supernatural virtue of *charity*. The poet Dante, in a brilliant verse, says that heaven is nothing other than "to live in loving, necessarily."

...whom you have called (today)/ from this world to yourself: Exactly as in the Latin. The initiative is God's, who *calls* or summons us, that we may be one with him.

Grant that he (she) who was united with your Son in a death like his,/ may also be one with him in his Resurrection: Here we bind in one both the baptism of the departed, and his death, recalling the words of Saint Paul, "Are you unaware that we who were baptized into Christ Jesus were baptized into his death? We were indeed buried with him through baptism into death, so that, just as Christ was raised from the dead by the glory of the Father, we too might live in newness of life. For if we have grown into union with him through a death like his, we shall also be united with him in the resurrection" (Rom 6: 3-5). Our hope in the resurrection is our hope in Christ, that in our own persons we may be granted the grace of dying and rising again with him.

REMEMBER also our brothers and sisters
who have fallen asleep in the hope of the resurrection,
and all who have died in your mercy:

welcome them into the light of your face.
Have mercy on us all, we pray,
that with the Blessed Virgin Mary, Mother of God,
with the blessed Apostles,

and all the Saints who have pleased you throughout
  the ages,
we may merit to be coheirs to eternal life,
and may praise and glorify you
through your Son, Jesus Christ.

■ Through him, and with him, and in him,
O God, almighty Father,
in the unity of the Holy Spirit,
all glory and honor is yours,
for ever and ever.
■ ■ Amen.

Then follows the Communion Rite.

...and all who have died in your mercy: It is one thing to die, but another to die *in the mercy* of God, whom we have the confidence to approach in love, Christ having led our way back to the Father.

...welcome them into the light of your face: Again we are reminded that we derive our personhood from God, for Scripture instructs us: "Your face, LORD, do I seek" (Ps 27: 8, RSV). The face of God brings light: "O LORD, let the light of your countenance shine upon us" (Ps 4: 7).

...who have pleased you throughout the ages: God is more than a divine will. He is the divine lover of mankind. He wishes to bestow upon us what every loving child wishes to hear from his father: words of praise, such as were heard when Jesus was baptized by John: "This is my beloved Son, with whom I am well pleased" (Mt 3: 17).

...we may merit to be coheirs to eternal life: We recall the parable of the Prodigal Son, who is welcomed home by the father not that he may be a hired hand, but that he may resume again his full place as son and heir. So too the words of Saint Paul: "The Spirit itself bears witness with our spirit that we are children of God, and if children, then heirs, heirs of God and joint heirs with Christ, if only we suffer with him that we may be glorified with him" (Rom 8: 16-17).

Eucharistic Prayer III

You are indeed Holy, O Lord,
  and all you have created
rightly gives you praise,
for through your Son our Lord Jesus Christ,
by the power and working of the Holy Spirit,
you give life to all things and make them holy,
and you never cease to gather a people to yourself,
so that from the rising of the sun to its setting
a pure sacrifice may be offered to your name.

Therefore, O Lord, we humbly implore you:
by the same Spirit graciously make holy
these gifts we have brought to you for consecration,
that they may become the Body and ✠ Blood
of your Son our Lord Jesus Christ,

at whose command we celebrate these mysteries.

...you give life to all things and make them holy: The emphasis is not on an abstract quality, but on God's working within all things: he "vivifies" them and sanctifies them.

...so that from the rising of the sun to its setting: A startling turn of phrase, combining the ideas of both time and space, the day of the whole world's existence. So the Lord speaks through the prophet Malachi: "For from the rising of the sun, even to its setting,/ my name is great among the nations" (Mal 1: 11).

...a pure sacrifice: The offering is a *sacrifice*, a making-holy, not by our will but by the power of God, and it is perfect because it is *pure*, without spot, without sin.

...we humbly implore you: Our language of prayer should be rich, touching upon the many reasons why we pray, and our many relations to God. Here we *implore* God on our knees, as beggars crying out for assistance, that the gifts we bring may be *consecrated*.

...at whose command we celebrate these mysteries: Exactly as in the Latin. The Eucharist is a *mystery* of God's love. The word is not meant to suggest something deceptive, but rather a reality that bursts the bounds of human comprehension, and that acts in ways that we cannot see.

For on the night he was betrayed
he himself took bread,
and, giving you thanks, he said the blessing,
broke the bread and gave it to his disciples, saying:

Take this, all of you, and eat of it,
for this is my Body,
which will be given up for you.

In a similar way, when supper was ended,
he took the chalice,
and, giving you thanks, he said the blessing,
and gave the chalice to his disciples, saying:

Take this, all of you, and drink from it,
for this is the chalice of my Blood,
the Blood of the new and eternal covenant,
which will be poured out for you
  and for many
for the forgiveness of sins.

Do this in memory of me.

■ The mystery of faith.
■■ We proclaim your Death, O Lord,
and profess your Resurrection
until you come again.

...*he himself took bread:* The pronoun intensifies the action. Jesus commanded us to celebrate the mysteries of the Eucharist, but it was he himself who instituted the Sacrament, as it was he himself who underwent suffering and death on the cross.

Or:

■ ■ When we eat this Bread and drink this Cup,
we proclaim your Death, O Lord,
until you come again.

Or:

■ ■ Save us, Savior of the world,
for by your Cross and Resurrection
you have set us free.

THEREFORE, O Lord, as we celebrate the memorial
of the saving Passion of your Son,
his wondrous Resurrection
and Ascension into heaven,
and as we look forward to his second coming,
we offer you in thanksgiving
this holy and living sacrifice.

Look, we pray, upon the oblation of your Church
and, recognizing the sacrificial Victim by whose death
you willed to reconcile us to yourself,
grant that we, who are nourished
by the Body and Blood of your Son
and filled with his Holy Spirit,
may become one body, one spirit in Christ.

...as we celebrate the memorial/ of the saving Passion of your Son: We do more than call the Passion to mind. We place it at the heart of our beings, both as individuals and as a people whom the Lord has brought together for the feast. It is, moreover, a *saving Passion*, in Latin a *passio salutifera* or health-bringing Passion. What our Lord suffered on the cross, by the wounds in his flesh, and by the far more terrible wounds in his heart, knowing that he was rejected by the very people to whom he came, becomes for us in the miracle of God's grace a remedy for sin, a healing balm. So Isaiah says of the Suffering Servant: "By his stripes we were healed" (Is 53: 5).

...his wondrous Resurrection: All love of wisdom begins in wonder. The Resurrection here is presented as the event that astonishes us, that rouses us out of the everyday round of things we believe we know. See the words of the Easter psalm: "By the Lord has this been done;/ it is wonderful in our eyes" (Ps 118: 23).

...you willed to reconcile us to yourself: We keep in mind that the saving death and Resurrection of Jesus has come by the will of the Father, for as Jesus says, "A son cannot do anything on his own, but only what he sees his father doing" (Jn 5: 19).

Mᴀʏ ʜᴇ ᴍᴀᴋᴇ of us
an eternal offering to you,
so that we may obtain an inheritance with your elect,
especially with the most Blessed Virgin Mary,
   Mother of God,
with your blessed Apostles and glorious Martyrs
(with Saint N.: the Saint of the day or Patron Saint)
and with all the Saints,
on whose constant intercession in your presence
we rely for unfailing help.

Mᴀʏ ᴛʜɪs Sᴀᴄʀɪꜰɪᴄᴇ of our reconciliation,
we pray, O Lord,
advance the peace and salvation of all the world.
Be pleased to confirm in faith and charity
your pilgrim Church on earth,
with your servant N. our Pope and N. our Bishop,
the Order of Bishops, all the clergy,
and the entire people you have gained for your own.

Listen graciously to the prayers of this family,
whom you have summoned before you:
in your compassion, O merciful Father,
gather to yourself all your children
scattered throughout the world.

…an inheritance with your elect: Literally, *your chosen ones,* the saints. The prophet Isaiah used the phrase to describe the faithful remnant of the Israelites who would be saved: "And I will bring forth a seed out of Jacob, and out of Judah an inheritor of my mountains:/ and mine elect shall inherit it" (Is 65: 9, KJV). The phrase still applies to us, for, as Jesus says, "For many are called, but few are chosen" (Mt 22: 14, RSV). This does not mean that God predetermines who shall be saved and who shall be damned, but that our salvation comes wholly from God, if we would but accept it. Says Jesus to his disciples, "You have not chosen me, but I have chosen you" (Jn 15: 16, KJV), and Saint John, "In this is love: not that we have loved God, but that he loved us" (1 Jn 4: 10).

Listen graciously to the prayers of this family: The Lord knows all that we do. When we ask him to listen to our prayers, we seek also his freely given favor, his grace.

…scattered throughout the world: When the Jews had sinned against the Law of God, believing that the presence of the Temple in Jerusalem would safeguard them from their enemies, the Lord gave them up to conquest, and they were *dispersed* throughout the world. In Christ, the command is now to preach the kingdom of God to the ends of the earth. That is no punishment, but the wondrous fulfillment of the words of the prophet. The new Zion, the Church, draws all people to her: "Nations shall walk by your light,/ and kings by your shining radiance" (Is 60: 3).

To OUR DEPARTED brothers and sisters
and to all who were pleasing to you
at their passing from this life,
give kind admittance to your kingdom.
There we hope to enjoy for ever the fullness
   of your glory

through Christ our Lord,
through whom you bestow on the world
   all that is good.

■■ Through him, and with him, and in him,
O God, almighty Father,
in the unity of the Holy Spirit,
all glory and honor is yours,
for ever and ever.
■■ Amen.

Then follows the Communion Rite.

...at their passing from this life: Literally, this *age* or *generation*. We leave the world of time, wherein things age and decay, and hope to enter the kingdom beyond all time, where we may enjoy for ever *the fullness* of the glory of God, as those who feast their fill, yet at a feast for ever fresh and new.

When this Eucharistic Prayer is used in Masses for the Dead,
the following may be said:

REMEMBER your servant N.
whom you have called (today)
from this world to yourself.
Grant that he (she) who was united with your Son
  in a death like his,
may also be one with him in his Resurrection,
when from the earth
he will raise up in the flesh those who have died,
and transform our lowly body
after the pattern of his own glorious body.
To our departed brothers and sisters, too,
and to all who were pleasing to you
at their passing from this life,
give kind admittance to your kingdom.
There we hope to enjoy for ever the fullness
  of your glory,
when you will wipe away every tear from our eyes.
For seeing you, our God, as you are,
we shall be like you for all the ages
and praise you without end,
through Christ our Lord,
through whom you bestow on the world
  all that is good.

...when from the earth/ he will raise up in the flesh those who have died: When Saint Paul preached to the men of Athens, they were ready to believe what he said about Christ, until he came to the truth that we, like Christ, will be raised up *in the flesh*. The body is no mere shell for the soul, to be cast aside. It is itself holy, and the grace of God sanctifies all of our works performed through the body. Our resurrection in the flesh is but a part of the promise of God, to create a new heaven and a new earth.

...when you will wipe away every tear from our eyes: Echoing the words of Christ, in the revelation to John: "Behold, God's dwelling is with the human race. He will dwell with them and they will be his people and God himself will always be with them [as their God]. He will wipe every tear from their eyes, and there shall be no more death or mourning, wailing or pain, [for] the old order has passed away" (Rv 21: 3-4). We are meant not simply to think of sadness, but of a real person, in the flesh, shedding real tears; and to imagine the very hand of Jesus, brushing away the tear, and welcoming us into joy.

...we shall be like you: This affirmation is restored to its context. We cannot, as we are now, see God, for as the Apostle John says in his Gospel, "No one has ever seen God. The only Son, God, who is at the Father's side, has revealed him" (Jn 1: 18). But we are promised more. "Beloved, we are God's children now; what we shall be has not yet been revealed. We do know that when it is revealed we shall be like him, for we shall see him as he is" (1 Jn 3: 2).

Eucharistic Prayer IV

IT IS TRULY right to give you thanks,
truly just to give you glory, Father most holy,
for you are the one God living and true,
existing before all ages and abiding for all eternity,
dwelling in unapproachable light;
yet you, who alone are good, the source of life,
have made all that is,
so that you might fill your creatures with blessings
and bring joy to many of them by the glory of
    your light.

And so, in your presence are countless hosts
    of Angels,
who serve you day and night
and, gazing upon the glory of your face,
glorify you without ceasing.

With them we, too, confess your name in exultation,
giving voice to every creature under heaven,
as we acclaim:

HOLY, Holy, Holy LORD God of hosts.
Heaven and earth are full of your glory.
Hosanna in the highest.
Blessed is he who comes in the name of the Lord.
Hosanna in the highest.

WE give you praise, Father most holy,
    for you are great
and you have fashioned all your works
in wisdom and in love.

You formed man in your own image
and entrusted the whole world to his care,

so that in serving you alone, the Creator,
he might have dominion over all creatures.
And when through disobedience he had lost
  your friendship,

you did not abandon him to the domain of death.

...in wisdom and in love: It is one thing to say that all creatures *show* God's wisdom and love. This phrase says more. It says that God fashioned them *in* wisdom and love, that is, that they owe the entirety of their beings, how they are and what they are and that they are, to the Word and the Spirit, the wisdom and the love of the Father. "For you love all things that are/ and loathe nothing that you have made" (Wis 11: 24).

...and entrusted the whole world to his care: The dominion of man over creation was to reflect the dominion of God, whose love brought all things into being. Man was to take *care* for things, and not simply use them for his own purposes, nor to suppose, as did our first parents, that the natural world could provide us with a salvation and a power apart from God.

...serving you alone: The adverb is crucial. God gave to man the surpassing dignity of dominion over all things, serving him *alone*, in whose service we grow like unto him. Recall the words of Jesus, when Satan offered to him all the kingdoms of the world, if only he would do him homage: "It is written: 'The Lord, your God, shall you worship/ and him alone shall you serve'" (Mt 4: 10).

...the domain of death: The word suggests a realm of command. In sin we lost our dominion, and now a new "ruler" comes to lord it over us. But God would not abandon us to that ruler, for, as Saint Paul says, now that Christ has risen from the dead, "Death no longer has dominion over him" (Rom 6: 9, RSV).

For you came in mercy to the aid of all,
so that those who seek might find you.
Time and again you offered them covenants
and through the prophets
taught them to look forward to salvation.

And you so loved the world, Father most holy,
that in the fullness of time

you sent your Only Begotten Son to be our Savior.

Made incarnate by the Holy Spirit
and born of the Virgin Mary,

he shared our human nature
in all things but sin.
To the poor he proclaimed the good news
    of salvation,
to prisoners, freedom,
and to the sorrowful of heart, joy.

...you came in mercy to the aid of all: The emphasis is upon the divine mercy. We must keep in mind that God has taken pity upon us, as a loving father pities a wayward son. We were once foolish and disobedient, says Saint Paul, living in malice and envy, but then "the kindness and generous love/ of God our savior appeared,/ not because of any righteous deeds we had done/ but because of his mercy" (Ti 3: 4-5).

...your Only Begotten Son: The Trinity is the central tenet of our faith, and here again we affirm that the Son is no creature, but is God himself, *begotten*, not made. It is that second Person of the Trinity, *begotten* of the Father before all ages, who becomes flesh and dwells among us.

Made incarnate by the Holy Spirit: The Incarnation occurred at his conception in the womb of Mary. What is stressed by the word "incarnate" is that Jesus took upon himself our *flesh*. We can therefore never suppose that flesh is a mere husk to be discarded in death. It too is meant to be sanctified, for, as Saint Paul says, "Do you not know that your body is a temple of the holy Spirit within you?" (1 Cor 6: 19).

...he shared our human nature/ in all things but sin: That is, he shared the condition of our life in the world, as creatures composed of body and soul. He felt cold and hunger, grief and disappointment, joy and contentment, as we do. He can therefore "sympathize with our weaknesses," for he too has been "tested in every way, yet without sin" (Heb 4: 15).

To accomplish your plan,
he gave himself up to death,
and, rising from the dead,
he destroyed death and restored life.

And that we might live no longer for ourselves
but for him who died and rose again for us,
he sent the Holy Spirit from you, Father,

as the first fruits for those who believe,

so that, bringing to perfection his work in the world,
he might sanctify creation to the full.

To accomplish your plan: The emphasis here is upon the providential plan of God, as Jesus is the fulfillment of the entire history of salvation.

...but for him who died and rose again for us: The clause is restored. We live for Christ, precisely because of what he has done for us. It is our loving response to his gift of love. "For whether we live, we live unto the Lord; and whether we die, we die unto the Lord: whether we live therefore, or die, we are the Lord's. For to this end Christ both died, and rose, and revived, that he might be Lord both of the dead and the living" (Rom 14: 8-9, KJV).

...as the first fruits for those who believe: The Latin recalls the sacrifice of the just man Abel, who gave of the *first fruits* of his labor in his sacrifice to God, and also the words of Saint Paul, who reminds us that Jesus is the *first fruit* of salvation: "For just as in Adam all die, so too in Christ shall all be brought to life; but each one in proper order: Christ the first fruits; then, at his coming, those who belong to Christ" (1 Cor 15: 22-23). So too the Holy Spirit is the gift God gives us, and the fruit of that gift; in the Holy Spirit we give back to God the first fruits of our devotion.

...bringing to perfection his work in the world: To *bring to perfection* is more than to complete. It is to fulfill. A creature, unlike God, does not possess his being all at once. We dwell in a world of becoming. The Incarnation of Christ does more than save mankind; it brings the world to *perfection, sanctifying creation to the full.*

Therefore, O Lord, we pray:
may this same Holy Spirit
graciously sanctify these offerings,
that they may become
the Body and ✠ Blood of our Lord Jesus Christ
for the celebration of this great mystery,
which he himself left us
as an eternal covenant.

For when the hour had come
for him to be glorified by you, Father most holy,
having loved his own who were in the world,

he loved them to the end:
and while they were at supper,
he took bread, blessed and broke it,
and gave it to his disciples, saying:

> Take this, all of you, and eat of it,
> for this is my Body,
> which will be given up for you.

For when the hour had come: We do not order our work on earth by mere time, but by the *hour*: of rising, and eating, and working, and taking repose. Christians pray the office of the *hours*, recalling at the proper hour of the day or the night the fitting events in the history of salvation. And when Jesus was drawing near to his ultimate sacrifice, he said, "The hour has come for the Son of Man to be glorified" (Jn 12: 23).

...he loved them to the end: Jesus showed us the depth of his love by loving us *to the end*, that is, to the end of his life, but to the *end* or completion of our redemption: "Before the feast of Passover, Jesus knew that his hour had come to pass from this world to the Father. He loved his own in the world and he loved them to the end" (Jn 13: 1).

IN A SIMILAR WAY,
taking the chalice filled with the fruit of the vine,
he gave thanks,
and gave the chalice to his disciples, saying:

> TAKE THIS, ALL OF YOU, AND DRINK FROM IT,
> FOR THIS IS THE CHALICE OF MY BLOOD,
> THE BLOOD OF THE NEW AND ETERNAL COVENANT,
> WHICH WILL BE POURED OUT FOR YOU
>   AND FOR MANY
> FOR THE FORGIVENESS OF SINS.
>
> DO THIS IN MEMORY OF ME.

He shows the chalice to the people, places it on the corporal,
and genuflects in adoration.

■ The mystery of faith.

And the people continue, acclaiming:

■ ■ We proclaim your Death, O Lord,
and profess your Resurrection
until you come again.

Or:

■ ■ When we eat this Bread and drink this Cup,
we proclaim your Death, O Lord,
until you come again.

Or:

■ ■ Save us, Savior of the world,
for by your Cross and Resurrection
you have set us free.

...*the fruit of the vine:* Wine, of course; but the words recall those at the offertory, when we ask the Lord to accept the *fruit of the vine* and the work of human hands. We remember too the parable: "I am the vine," says Jesus, "you are the branches" (Jn 15: 5).

THEREFORE, O Lord,
as we now celebrate the memorial of
our redemption,
we remember Christ's Death
and his descent to the realm of the dead,

we proclaim his Resurrection
and his Ascension to your right hand,
and, as we await his coming in glory,
we offer you his Body and Blood,
the sacrifice acceptable to you
which brings salvation to the whole world.

Look, O Lord, upon the Sacrifice
which you yourself have provided for your Church,

and grant in your loving kindness
to all who partake of this one Bread and one Chalice
that, gathered into one body by the Holy Spirit,
they may truly become a living sacrifice in Christ

to the praise of your glory.

...we remember Christ's Death: Literally, in the Latin, we *cultivate* the memorial of his death, as if we were tilling the soil of our souls, that they might bear good fruit. It is something more than recall. It is the opposite of a sinful and negligent *forgetting:* we make the memory of the Death and Resurrection of Jesus the fruitful heart of our worship and our lives.

...we proclaim his Resurrection: We desire to obey the words of Jesus. It is a good thing to remember his glorious victory, but a better thing to *proclaim* it. For what we have been given, we should give freely in return, and proclaim the name of Jesus from the housetops (Lk 12: 3).

...which you yourself have provided for your Church: Again we note the marvelous truth, that it is God *himself* who has *provided,* or prepared from the foundations of the world, the very sacrifice which we offer to him. He, the God of love, is king and priest and sacrifice.

...and grant in your loving kindness: We acknowledge in gratitude the grace and mercy of our God. It is his *loving kindness* that allows us to be *gathered into one body by the Holy Spirit,* making of us what on our own we could never be, a *living sacrifice in Christ.* The wording is meant to be precise here. All victims on the altars of old are slain. Christ is the one and the only sacrifice that brings life, and if we too offer ourselves, *in Christ,* as the mystical Body of Christ, we will share in his life.

...to the praise of your glory: We praise God most of all not for what he has done for us, but for who he is, the God whose very being shines forth in glory.

THEREFORE, Lord, remember now
all for whom we offer this sacrifice:
especially your servant N. our Pope,
N. our Bishop, and the whole Order of Bishops,
all the clergy,
those who take part in this offering,
those gathered here before you,
your entire people,
and all who seek you with a sincere heart.

Remember also
those who have died in the peace of your Christ
and all the dead,
whose faith you alone have known.

To ALL OF US, your children,
grant, O merciful Father,
that we may enter into a heavenly inheritance
with the Blessed Virgin Mary, Mother of God,
and with your Apostles and Saints in your kingdom.
There, with the whole of creation,
freed from the corruption of sin and death,
may we glorify you through Christ our Lord,
through whom you bestow on the world
  all that is good.

■ Through him, and with him, and in him,
O God, almighty Father,
in the unity of the Holy Spirit,
all glory and honor is yours,
for ever and ever.

■■ Amen.

...*and the whole Order of Bishops:* The phrase means more than *every bishop.* We thank God here for the *Order* of Bishops, the teaching and protective office and all the men who hold it, overseeing the shepherds and their flocks. Jesus taught that among the pagans, rulers would cloak their ambition under the guise of being "Benefactors" (Lk 22: 25), but he wishes those who are charged with great responsibility to be the servants of all the rest, for "the last will be first, and the first will be last" (Mt 20: 16).

...*in the peace of your Christ:* The pronoun is touching, expressive of love and oneness. Jesus is the *Christ* or the *anointed* of the Father.

...*through whom you bestow on the world all that is good:* The action of the word is greater than we can possibly know. Indeed, Christ has come to dwell with us, to share our humanity and raise us to his divinity, but it is also through the Word that all good things come to *the world,* all of creation, through all of time.

—————• THE COMMUNION RITE •—————

■ At the Savior's command
and formed by divine teaching,
we dare to say:

O UR FATHER. . .

■ Deliver us, Lord, we pray, from every evil,
graciously grant peace in our days,
that, by the help of your mercy,
we may be always free from sin

and safe from all distress,
as we await the blessed hope
and the coming of our Savior, Jesus Christ.

■ ■ For the kingdom,
the power and the glory are yours
now and for ever.

At the Savior's command/ and formed by divine teaching,/ we dare to say: Jesus did not simply give us the words to pray with. He exhorted us, with a saving *command*, and *formed* us by instituting a new prayer. And therefore, as Saint Paul suggests, we do something audacious: "God sent the spirit of his Son into our hearts, crying out, 'Abba, Father!'" (Gal 4: 6).

…that, by the help of your mercy,/ we may be always free from sin: The meaning is slightly different from what is suggested by the flat and more general "keep us free from sin." We acknowledge here the *help* of God's mercy, as he supports us in our trials; yet we are the ones who must welcome this assistance. The little word "always," translating the Latin *semper*, suggests the whole drama of human life. It is one thing to say that someone is free from sin, but quite another to say that from day to day he relies upon the mercy of God, and, so strengthened, gains that freedom always.

…and safe from all distress: The Latin suggests more than an emotional state. It is real *distress*, yet in the midst of the troubles of this life we beg to be *securi*, free of the harm that the troubles cause, *safe*.

■ Lord Jesus Christ,
who said to your Apostles:
Peace I leave you, my peace I give you,
look not on our sins,
but on the faith of your Church,
and graciously grant her peace and unity
in accordance with your will.

Who live and reign for ever and ever.
■■ Amen.

■ The peace of the Lord be with you always.
■■ And with your spirit.

Then, if appropriate, the Deacon, or the Priest, adds:

■ Let us offer each other the sign of peace.

Then the Priest takes the host, breaks it over the paten,
and places a small piece in the chalice,
saying quietly:

May this mingling of the Body and Blood
of our Lord Jesus Christ
bring eternal life to us who receive it.

Meanwhile the following is sung or said:

LAMB of God…

...and graciously grant her peace and unity/ in accordance with your will: Exactly as in the Latin. We do well to pray for more than ourselves; we pray for *the Church*, the Bride of Christ, and we repeat the petition in the Lord's Prayer, submitting our desires to the *will* of God.

Who live and reign for ever and ever: The second verb is restored to its rightful place. If Christ should live for ever, but not *reign*, that would be of no avail to us. We recall the image of Christ seated upon the throne, and the cry of the angel of the seventh trumpet: "The kingdom of the world now belongs to our Lord and to his Anointed, and he will reign forever and ever" (Rv 11: 15).

Then the Priest, with hands joined, says quietly:

Lord Jesus Christ, Son of the living God,
who, by the will of the Father
and the work of the Holy Spirit,
through your Death gave life to the world,
free me by this, your most holy Body and Blood,
from all my sins and from every evil;
keep me always faithful to your commandments,
and never let me be parted from you.

Or:

May the receiving of your Body and Blood,
Lord Jesus Christ,
not bring me to judgment and condemnation,

but through your loving mercy
be for me protection in mind and body
and a healing remedy.

...keep me always faithful to your commandments: Literally, make me to *cleave to your commandments*, for in them is truth and life. So says the Psalmist: "With all my heart I seek you;/ let me not stray from your commands" (Ps 119: 10).

...not bring me to judgment and condemnation: If we are *judged* by our own merits, we must fall, because we are all sinners, the children of Adam: "For after one sin there was the judgment that brought condemnation" (Rom 5: 16).

...protection in mind and body: That is, we beg the Lord to keep us safe, as a watchman at the gates, or the shepherd guarding his flock. Then the Eucharist, his own Body and Blood, will be for us *a healing remedy*. For none of us is healthy, as the Psalmist says: "There is no health in my flesh because of your indignation;/ there is no wholeness in my bones because of my sin" (Ps 38: 4). But Christ is the good Physician, who comes to make us whole.

■ Behold the Lamb of God,
behold him who takes away the sins of the world.

Blessed are those called to the supper of the Lamb.

Behold the Lamb of God: The prayer echoes the ringing words of the Baptist (Jn 1: 29) and also the words of Pontius Pilate as he presented Jesus to the people, scourged and crowned with thorns: "Behold, the man!" (Jn 19: 5). The repeated call to *behold* the Lamb of God is more than a declaration that the bread and wine have become the Body and Blood of Jesus. It is a call to *contemplate* the mystery, to *gaze* upon it, to *behold* with gratitude what God has done for us. Confronted with incomparable beauty, we recognize its distance from us, but we cross that very distance in the act of *beholding*, which is an act of love.

Blessed are those called to the supper of the Lamb: The repetition of "Lamb" links the words of John the Baptist above with the words of the angel in Revelation: "Blessed are those who have been called to the wedding feast of the Lamb" (Rv 19: 9).

And together with the people the Priest adds once:

■■ Lord, I am not worthy
that you should enter under my roof,
but only say the word
and my soul shall be healed.

The Priest then says quietly:

May the Body of Christ
keep me safe for eternal life.

And he reverently consumes the Body of Christ.

Then he takes the chalice and says quietly:

May the Blood of Christ
keep me safe for eternal life.

And he reverently consumes the Blood of Christ.

After this, he takes the paten or ciborium and approaches the communicants. The Priest raises a host slightly and shows it to each of the communicants, saying:

■ The Body of Christ.

The communicant replies:

■■ Amen.

And receives Holy Communion.

Lord, I am not worthy/ that you should enter under my roof,/ but only say the word/ and my soul shall be healed: These are – with one crucial exception – the exact words of the centurion, whose beloved servant was dying (Mt 8: 8). When Jesus offered to enter his house, he uttered this declaration of obedience, faith, and humility. "For I am a man under authority" (Mt 8: 9, RSV), he said, remarking that when he in turn ordered a soldier to go, he went, or to do this, and he did. The analogy is clear. Jesus need only *say the word*, and the servant will be healed. The man is too abashed to see Jesus submit to his hospitality. We, however, are granted the great grace of the Eucharist, wherein Jesus indeed *does enter under our roof*. His is the initiative, not ours. We do not receive him, so much as he comes to us despite the lowliness of our dwelling place. And what beneath our roofs lies ill? No mere *servant* now, but our very *souls*.

May the Body of Christ/ keep me safe for eternal life: The image is again of a guard. The priest is like a man on pilgrimage to the heavenly City, who must be guarded against the dangers of the journey.

keep me safe

*Then the Priest purifies the paten over the chalice
and also the chalice itself.*

While he carries out the purification, the Priest says quietly:

What has passed our lips as food, O Lord,
may we possess in purity of heart,
that what has been given to us in time
may be our healing for eternity.

A sacred silence may be observed for a while.

When the Communion Rite is finished, the Priest says:

■ Let us pray.

*All pray in silence with the Priest for a while, unless silence has just
been observed. Then the Priest says the Prayer after Communion,
at the end of which the people acclaim:*

■■ Amen.

What has passed our lips as food, O Lord: Again, the words bring to our attention the flesh, the body. Jesus came not to save disembodied human souls, but the human person in his wholeness, body and soul together. Recall the astonishment of the disciples when the risen Christ invited them to sit with him at a meal of a broiled fish (Jn 21: 9-13).

...that what has been given to us in time/ may be our healing for eternity: The balance of the clauses is perfect and beautiful. Now we dwell *in time*, and receive the gift of the Eucharist here, in this church, on this particular day, but we pray that this moment of grace will make us whole for *eternity*, that is the dwelling place of God, who suffers no past and awaits no future, but simply *is*.

THE CONCLUDING RITES

■ The Lord be with you.
■ ■ **And with your spirit.**

■ May almighty God bless you,
the Father, and the Son, ✠ and the Holy Spirit.
■ ■ **Amen.**

The Deacon, or the Priest, then dismisses the people saying:

• FORM A •

■ Go forth, the Mass is ended.

Go forth, the Mass is ended: The order of the verbs is as in the Latin. The word we translate as "Mass," *missa,* suggests a sending-forth. We are not so much dismissed *from* Mass as *sent forth* for the proclamation of what we have just heard and witnessed. This fact is stressed by two of the alternate dismissals: *Go and announce the Gospel of the Lord,* and *Go in peace, glorifying the Lord by your life.* These dismissals make apostles of us all, to the *glory* of the Lord, for he has granted us the consummate favor of allowing his radiance to shine forth in our words and deeds, so long as we dedicate all that we do, even in our most ordinary works from day to day, to him. We are perhaps too used to the word "Mass" as signifying only what has just transpired within the walls of the church. Instead we might do well to hear the clarion call ringing in the Latin: "Go forth, for you are sent forth, you are missionaries," and as we accept that commission we know that the Mass is never ended, but is always beginning anew, until the Lord shall come again.

• FORM B •

■ Go and announce the Gospel of the Lord.

Go and announce the Gospel of the Lord: This alternate dismissal stresses the role of the laity in the evangelization of the world. "Go into the whole world," says Jesus to the disciples after his Resurrection, "and proclaim the gospel to every creature" (Mk 16: 15). The word "gospel" is, in its ancient English meaning, the *good spell* or good tidings, exactly as in the original Greek *evangelion*. When Jesus was born in Bethlehem, no one in the countryside would have known of it, had not the heralds of the Lord, the *angels,* brought the tidings to the shepherds. Now the Resurrection of Jesus, the great victory over sin and death, is made known to the world by messengers again, by *evangels,* as all Christians are called to be. "Come and see," we cry out, "what the Lord has done!"

• FORM C •

■ Go in peace, glorifying the Lord by your life.

• FORM D •

■ Go in peace.

■■ Thanks be to God.

Go in peace, glorifying the Lord by your life: So Saint Paul exhorts us: "Whatever you do, do everything for the glory of God" (1 Cor 10: 31). So too he prays for his disciples in Thessalonica, that they may so live that "the name of our Lord Jesus may be glorified" in them, and they in Christ (2 Thes 1: 12). Every moment of our lives is an opportunity to give God that glory; when we rejoice, when we mourn, when we leap with youth and strength, and when we lay ourselves down to die. All times, all places, before all people, and in all our deeds, we may preach with our lives, proclaiming, "Not to us, O LORD, not to us/ but to your name give glory/ because of your kindness, because of your truth" (Ps 115: 1). It is a glory of love that brims over, that blesses us, for it is as Jesus says to his Apostles, praying and giving glory to the Father: "I have given them the glory you gave me, so that they may be one, as we are one, I in them and you in me, that they may be brought to perfection as one, that the world may know that you sent me, and that you loved them even as you loved me" (Jn 17: 22-23). To God be the glory, now and for ever.

MAGNIFICAT Roman Missal Companion

Publisher: **Pierre-Marie Dumont**
Editor-in-Chief: **Peter John Cameron, O.P.**
Senior Editor: **Romanus Cessario, O.P.**
Contributors: **Archbishop J. Augustine Di Noia, O.P.,**
Father Bernard Mulcahy, O.P., and Anthony Esolen
Managing Editor: **Catherine Kolpak**
Editorial Assistant: **Andrew Matt**
Administrative Assistants: **Jeanne Shanahan, Nora Macagnone**
Senior Managing Editor: **Frédérique Chatain**
Iconography: **Isabelle Mascaras**
Cover: **Solange Bosdevesy**
Permissions: **Diaga Seck-Rauch**
Proofreader: **Janet Chevrier**
Layout: **Élise Borel**
Deputy Publisher: **Romain Lizé**

Acknowledgments

Some Scripture selections are taken from the *New American Bible with Revised New Testament*, copyright © 1991, 1986, 1970 by the Confraternity of Christian Doctrine, 3211 Fourth St., N.E., Washington, DC. 20017-1194, and are used by license of the copyright owner. All rights reserved. No part of the *New American Bible* may be reproduced in any form without permission in writing from the copyright owner.

Some Scripture selections are taken from *The Holy Bible: Revised Standard Version, Catholic Edition,* copyright 1946 (New Testament), copyright 1952 (Old Testament), copyright 1957 (The Apocrypha), copyright 1965 (The Catholic Edition of the New Testament), © 1966 (The Catholic Edition of the Old Testament, incorporating the Apocrypha) by Division of Christian Education of the National Council of Churches of Christ in the United States of America.

Excerpts from the English translation of *The Roman Missal* © 2010, International Commission on English in the Liturgy Corporation. All rights reserved.

The trademark MAGNIFICAT depicted in this publication is used under license from and is the exclusive property of Magnificat Central Service Team, Inc., A Ministry to Catholic Women, and may not be used without its written consent.

Published with the approval of the Committee on Divine Worship of the United States Conference of Catholic Bishops.

© MAGNIFICAT USA LLC, New York, 2011.

Printed in Canada by Transcontinental.

Cover: *Christ Blessing* (c. 1500), Giovanni Battista Cima da Conegliano (c. 1459-1517), Gemäldegalerie Alte Meister, Dresden, Germany. © Staatliche Kunstsammlungen Dresden / Bridgeman Giraudon.

Biography of Professor Anthony Esolen

Anthony Esolen, professor of English at Providence College, is the translator and annotator of a three-volume verse edition of Dante's *Divine Comedy* (Random House), of the great Catholic Reformation epic by Torquato Tasso, *Jerusalem Delivered* (Johns Hopkins), and of the ancient philosophical epic by the Latin poet Lucretius, *On the Nature of Things* (Johns Hopkins). He has also translated over one hundred Psalms from the Vulgate Latin for a new psalter to be published by Baronius Press, and several of the great Anglo-Saxon elegies of the early Church in England, including the powerful *Dream of the Rood*. Professor Esolen is the author of several books, including *Ironies of Faith: The Laughter at the Heart of Christian Literature* (Intercollegiate Studies Institute Press), a book of literary criticism, and *The Story of Jesus, The Story of the Christian Life* (Our Sunday Visitor Press). He has published over a hundred essays on Sacred Scripture, the spiritual life, and Christian art in various journals, among them *First Things, This Rock, Catholic World Report*, and *Touchstone: A Journal of Mere Christianity*, where he also serves as a senior editor. Professor Esolen has been a regular contributor to MAGNIFICAT since 2007. He, his wife Debra, and their two children Jessica and David worship at Sacred Heart Church, West Warwick, Rhode Island.

If you liked THE MAGNIFICAT ROMAN MISSAL COMPANION you will love MAGNIFICAT

If you would like to continue each month to deepen your understanding and appreciation of the new translation of the Mass…

> MAGNIFICAT *is the answer.*

If you would like to receive regularly each month a resource that would help you to develop your prayer life…

> MAGNIFICAT *is the answer.*

If you would like to have a companion to accompany you each day in the growth of your spiritual life…

> MAGNIFICAT *is the answer.*

If you would like to benefit from a worship aid that helps you participate in the Holy Mass with greater fervor…

> MAGNIFICAT *is the answer.*

If you desire to find a way to a more profound love for Our Blessed Savior…

We invite you to become part of the growing worldwide MAGNIFICAT family.

MAGNIFICAT borrows its title from the words that Our Blessed Lady spoke when, already pregnant with the infant Christ, she visited her cousin Elizabeth and exclaimed: "My soul magnifies the Lord, and my spirit rejoices in God my Savior, for he has regarded the low estate of his handmaiden" (Lk 1: 46-48).

AN ANNUAL SUBSCRIPTION TO MAGNIFICAT

promises thirteen issues — one per month with a special issue for Holy Week — filled with spiritual insight, exquisite art, and invaluable inspiration. You will discover the most beautiful prayers, readings, and hymns of the Church in this lavishly printed, easy-to-read, pocket-sized worship aid. MAGNIFICAT provides a fitting way to enter fully into the Church's liturgical rhythms and spiritual legacy.